A
Calm
Fire

THE SWISS LIST

Philippe
Jaccottet

A
Calm
Fire
and
other
travel
writings

TRANSLATED BY
JOHN TAYLOR

LONDON NEW YORK CALCUTTA

swiss arts council
prohelvetia

This publication has
been supported by a
grant from Pro Helvetia,
Swiss Arts Council

PAP
TAGORE
www.bibliofrance.in

The work is published
with the support of the
Publication Assistance
Programmes of the
Institut français

Seagull Books, 2019

Originally published in French as: Philippe Jaccottet, *Libretto* ©
Éditions La Dogana 1990; *Cristal et fumée* © Éditions Fata
Morgana 1993; *À partir du mot Russie* © Éditions Fata Morgana
2002; *Israël, cahier bleu* © Éditions Fata Morgana 2004; *Un calme
Feu* © Éditions Fata Morgana 2007; *Libretto* and *À partir du mot
Russie* are included in *Oeuvres* (Gallimard-Pléiade, 2014).

First published in English translation by Seagull Books, 2019
English translation © John Taylor, 2019

ISBN   978 0 8574 2 598 0

British Library Cataloguing-in-Publication Data
A catalogue record for this book is available from the British
Library.

Typeset by Seagull Books, Calcutta, India
Printed and bound by Hyam Enterprises, Calcutta, India

CONTENTS

This book offers the first English translation of the travel writings of the Swiss poet Philippe Jaccottet (b. 1925). For admirers of the poetry who are little aware of the man's personal life—and Jaccottet is very discreet—these writings are not only engaging but also instructive. The poet, who is also an esteemed translator (from several languages) and a penetrating literary essayist, has long had the reputation of living in relative isolation, even in a certain solitude, ever since 1953 in a village—Grignan—in the southern French Alps. Now and then a book reviewer or an academic critic even goes so far as to describe him as the 'hermit of Grignan'. Although he has indeed long lived in Grignan, these pieces, most of which are short evocations or narratives, show that the author of *La Promenade sous les arbres* (Walking under the Trees, 1957) has often travelled abroad. Moreover, he's no loner. His early trips to Italy were often taken in the company of youthful friends and his later trips to that country and several others have usually been taken not only with his wife, the artist Anne-Marie Jaccottet, but also with relatives (such as Henri and Suzanne Jaccottet) or close friends (such as Michel and Louki Rossier or Gérard and Marie Khoury). Camaraderie and friendship are integral elements of his approach to travel and they are befittingly celebrated here.

As revealed by these five volumes, Jaccottet began travelling as a budding poet in early adulthood and never stopped. Published in 1990, *Libretto* was long in the making, but it recalls trips taken to Italy that date back to the postwar years, 1946 to 1948, when he'd just finished his undergraduate studies (in philosophy, German and Ancient Greek) at the University of Lausanne. Jaccottet began working on the manuscript of *Libretto* some two decades later, in 1966/1967, and then, after another long break, in 1976. Several other trips to Italy had taken place in the meantime, including sojourns in Rome to work on his translations of Giuseppe Ungaretti's poetry with the Italian poet himself. These Italian trips were especially formative and, arguably, profoundly affected the thematic and even stylistic orientation of his *oeuvre*.

Crystal and Smoke (1993) was similarly slow in taking shape. The book collects prose texts based on a trip taken to Spain in March–April 1978, a first trip to Greece in May 1978 (followed by a second in autumn 1981), as well as, finally, a trip to Egypt in February 1992. But there was already a long stay on the island of Majorca, from May to July 1958, when Jaccottet translated St John of the Cross and Luis de Góngora. Whereas his lifelong engagement with the works of Rilke and Hölderlin appears self-evident, given the themes of his own writing, his interest in Góngora's Baroque poetry can seem less obvious; but several passages in these travel writings elucidate an unexpected and fruitful proximity.

A little more than a year after the Egyptian trip, the Jaccottets travelled to Israel (in April 1993), which inspired, a decade later, *Israel: Blue Notebook* (2004). And only a month after the publication of that volume, they were travelling in Lebanon and Syria in October–November 2004, a trip evoked in *A Calm Fire* (2007). Whereas *Beginning with the Word 'Russia'* (2002) consists of three essays with a much more literary focus, the poet took a trip—after the essays had been written—to Moscow and Saint Petersburg in May 1996; and the essays often study the relationship that Russian authors such as Fyodor Dostoyevsky, Anton Chekhov and Osip Mandelstam entertain with landscape, even as Jaccottet simultaneously explores his own imaginative visions of Russia as gleaned through his reading of their work and other Russian classics, not to mention Jules Verne's novel *Michel Strogoff*. Similarly, the poet confronts the lifelong mental imagery acquired through his childhood reading of a favourite book, *The Thousand and One Nights* (with its marvellous illustrations), to what he comes across in the Middle East. In other words, during the six decades when Jaccottet was putting together his collections of poetry and, increasingly, of poetic prose, as well as doing an extraordinary amount of translation and not a little book reviewing, he was also garnering subject matter, from his several trips, for these volumes of travel pieces.

This is not to forget Jaccottet's only commissioned 'travel book', about Austria (*Autriche*, 1961), not translated here, nor the settings of some of his personal writing: *Éléments d'un songe* (Elements of a Dream, 1961) alludes to a stay in the Balearic Islands; a few memories of another trip to Italy appear in *L'Effraie* (The Barn-Owl, 1953); and *Les Cormorans* (The Cormorants, 1980) is based on the memory of a trip to Holland in July–August 1972.

The detailing of these trips would remain mostly anecdotal, were it not for the necessary corrective that they provide with respect to the poet's reputation of being a reclusive man—a romantic image of the lonely poet that is clearly, as these pages reveal, a misrepresentation. More importantly, these 'marginal' travel writings cast light on the philosophical outlook that he develops, implicitly, in his poetry and especially his poetic prose. His poetic prose texts often focus on landscapes around Grignan (the Lez stream, Larche Pass) or on elements of nature (cherry trees, peonies, violets, wild carrots, bindweed, robins, nightingales). Although the travel writings emphasize foreign towns and monuments, and occasionally the toils of tourism, they also offer observations of nature in these different settings, with Jaccottet's central concern, 'light', remaining as essential as ever. The frequency with which colours are defined, not to mention natural leitmotifs such as 'water' and 'air', show how these essays complement the personal writing of the poet of *Airs* (1967) and the prose writer of—to mention a small recent book—*Couleur de terre* (Earth Colour, 2009).

An additional nuance must be made. There was a 'turn', though not an entirely strict one, in Jaccottet's work beginning with *Cahier de verdure* (Notebook of Greenery, 1990), upon which verse poetry was mostly abandoned in favour of poetic prose. Prose thereafter enabled him to deepen certain themes already expressed in his poetry; the questioning that was already at the heart of his verse evocations became more explicit and elaborate. The poet in fact underscores this shift. For example, in *A Calm Fire*, mentioning Palmyra, he confesses in parentheses: '(A long time ago, maybe I'd have known how to say [what I'm seeing] in a single weightless poem, but I've lost the secret or the key—that no hand will ever tender to you again.)'

Although it's true that the prose of the travel writings is very different from the verse written by Jaccottet in the 1950–1990 period, at least some passages here aren't far removed, in tone and even in subject matter—which is by no means exclusively the specificities of 'place'—from the later poetic prose texts included in *Notebook of Greenery* as well as *Après beaucoup d'années* (After Many Years, 1994), *Et, néanmoins* (And, Nonetheless, 2001) and *Ce peu de bruits* (These Slight Noises, 2008). The four travel books coming after the 'turn' of 1990—*Crystal and Smoke*, *Beginning with the Word 'Russia'*, *Israel: Blue Notebook* and *A Calm Fire*—show the same characteristic concerns: an individual's confrontation with the inevitability of his death, the possibilities and impossibilities of religious faith, the experience of (and scepticism about) sacredness, indeed the questioning of the comforting romantic imagery of transcendence in regard to our physical being in the world, on this earth. As a travel writer, Jaccottet constantly moves from what he has seen or sensed to these more philosophical considerations. Especially in the four books that followed *Libretto*, which is distinguished by its youthful spirit and narrative emphasis, Jaccottet seeks to get beyond the on-the-spot recording of happenstance and foreign idiosyncrasies and explore an individual's relationship to the fundamental issues of existing. And it mustn't be forgotten that *Libretto* and the other books exude a sensuousness that enables Jaccottet's reader to better understand the latent sensuality, even subtle eroticism, which crop up now and then in his poetry and especially his poetic prose.

Except for *Libretto* and *Beginning with the Word 'Russia'*, the French originals of which are now included in the magisterial Gallimard-Pléiade volume of Jaccottet's *Oeuvres* (2014), the travel writings translated here have been published in France (by Éditions Fata Morgana) without notes. (*Libretto* was first published in Switzerland by Éditions La Dogana.) I've elucidated as many cultural and literary allusions as possible, drawing on and adding to the Pléiade notes for the two aforementioned volumes and drafting my own for the other three books. What every reader will spot, from the onset, is the dichotomy, even tension, in Jaccottet between his literary, linguistic, artistic and musical knowledge, and the landscapes or monuments that he's 'glimpsing'—as he puts it with typical modesty. He has an inner drive towards reality *per se*—the desire to experience and then to evoke what he sees without passing it through the filter of learning; at the same time, he tests, against reality, what he has read and the mental images that books have given him.

In fact, much of his writing here is about imagery: how images are formed in him, how he dissects and reconsiders them, how he conscientiously formulates or re-formulates them in his writing, and their validity, their authenticity, their truth; or their soothing illusions and self-deceiving falsehoods. Jaccottet is finely attentive to the objects and phenomena of the world—the sand and stone and sunlight and shadow that he encounters during his travels—but he also wonders if one can go deeper into them, or beyond them. Wondering—and wonder—so fully nourish his writing that they become the very act of his writing, his poetics, as it were. His perceptions are often apperceptions; that is, if one thinks of this latter term as defined by Kant, Leibniz and Maine de Biran, he seeks to capture, to grasp, to record states of sensibility in which he's aware that he's in the process of perceiving, of feeling, of thinking—those moments when one suddenly feels oneself existing wholly in the world, a sentiment or a sensation of plenitude or presence or communion that must, in turn, be examined and reexamined—wondered about—through writing. At home or abroad, Jaccottet dwells on these privileged instants, meditating on their elusive deeper meaning (or their possible absence of deeper meaning) and thus on aliveness as well as on the difficulties of writing genuinely, 'honestly', about it: our being in the world, our living on the earth. Rarely have these issues been so sincerely and scrupulously and seriously dealt with in literature.

Saint-Barthélemy d'Anjou
30 November 2018

Libretto

PREFATORY NOTE

For more than twenty years, I've projected to devote a book to Italy in an attempt to settle a debt towards a country that I've long loved as one can love a living person, that is, by making excuses for his or her worst qualities and even finding charm in them. Every time I've taken up this initiative, I've given up more or less quickly thereafter. First, because I have a bad memory and only too belatedly and too rarely made up for this defect by taking notes. When I was young, it seemed unworthy of a poet to carry a notebook around, to account for his days like a miser. This was a mistake, but the qualm hasn't entirely left me. Moreover, evoking my memories is truly not my strong point, and I manage to do so only by more or less forcing myself to do so. Finally, I have to resign myself to admitting that I have only rarely been able to speak about those works of art, paintings, statues, churches, palaces and gardens that shine forth in Italy like lush sparkling fruit in a vast orchard.

It's now too late to work myself to the bone over this project. I'll thus content myself with this, indeed, very small book without sighing further or making additional comments. Most of the texts go back to my first trips, between 1946 and 1948; I haven't refrained from touching them up. The 'Postcards' are simple vignettes and, like 'Two Dawns', are much more recent.

RELIEFS

1946–1948

'Aranciate, uva, panini . . . '

To Gilbert Koull

It took place during the first days of September, 1946 . . . I have no wish to describe the circumstances of this first trip abroad after the war, only to point out that they were particularly happy ones: I'd finished my academic studies and just barely managed to slip out of military service; I knew that, upon my return, I'd settle in Paris and begin to work there almost without constraints; a whimsical companion full of good cheer was with me and also invited to Rome for more than a month by a young woman artist, a little older than we were, who had her studio there. What else needs to be added? It was a genuine casting off, a door opening as in dreams or fairy tales; the impatience, the expectation, the hope, the verve that wise men beckon us to recover every time we wake up, until the very end— but who can or would imitate this?

It took us nearly thirty-six hours to reach Rome from Lausanne. Most of the bridges had been destroyed and replaced by what appeared to be simple, breathtaking, one-track footbridges; so that a train, in order to pass another heading in the opposite direction, had to come to a halt for hours, either in the middle of the countryside or in stations that were also still in ruins. Naturally, those few trains were overcrowded, and I don't think that, for the entire journey, we were ever seated elsewhere than on our sorry-looking suitcases in aisles where you needed to perform acrobatics in order to squirm your way through. Most of the passengers were Italians: soldiers, women, ordinary people, low-level civil servants, as far as we could tell, that is, rather vaguely, since neither of us had the slightest notion of Italian. Well, this jostled, exhausted crowd all crammed together remained cheerful, patient and talkative. They kindly poked fun at us, at what they surmised of our adventure, our enthusiasm, our naivety. They offered us grapes.

And indeed I haven't forgotten, nor will ever forget, that once we'd crossed the border the first Italian words engraved in my ear formed a refrain heard in the middle of the night on every station platform: 'Aranciate, uva, panini . . . ', words that need to be transcribed as they were chanted every time: 'Aranciaaate, ouuva, paniiini . . . ' Today, still hearing them enveloped in night and soot, I have the impression that they were not only words but also the very things they evoked; that the words made those things shine in orange and gilded green among the bits of smoky grit blowing up against the train doors as if in a party (while the wounds of war remained so visible), almost like the lemons in Goethe's poem, which, initially, was too hackneyed and trivialized in its French translation, a poem in fact so beautiful that it long summed up nostalgia for Italy, the dream of heading south by means of the ambiguous Mignon's voice.

Even better: this whole first Roman sojourn would be engraved forever in me as this insignia of ripe fruit, of golden fruit against a background of dark hearty foliage; for even if we came from a country spared from the violence and devastation of the war, it had not entirely been spared by food rationing and, even less so for many of us, by anxiety and moral suffering. So that, perhaps naively and also superficially, what initially struck my companion and me in Rome was the plenitude, the opulence of the fruit displayed in the markets, the sumptuous richness of the cream deserts in the pastry-shop windows; to which responded, as in a musical score for woodwind and brass instruments, a polyphony of sensual tenderness and brightness, a brightness unafraid of extravagance: not only the building fronts and the swells, volutes and baroque exuberance of the stone but also the beauty of the servants and the saleswomen, themselves a mixture of milk, honey and night, to whom, as the perfect 'false simpletons from Sologne' (or, rather, a Swiss canton) we still were, we could only devote an admiration of gaping mouths or, almost, of outrageously shy wooers.

Via Appia

It's true that G. and I lacked seriousness. Count Giacinto, the composer, especially took it out on me while we were laughing about some new idiocy that had crossed our minds, and he said gravely: 'You don't seem very sensitive to the beauty of this place. When Goethe came onto the Via Appia, like you for the first time, he exclaimed: "This is where I was born!"—and you, you're making jokes!' I felt completely ill at ease: I was obviously not up to the task and horribly frivolous. Goethe . . . It was obvious that, like him, I should have leant on the tomb of Cecilia Metella (she whom the Count absolutely insisted was the monument of the Scipions) and felt inside me, if not a new birth, at least some great emotion. After all, it was G.'s fault, for he was incapable of respecting the sublime quality of the moment; also the fault of the driver who, convinced that we'd be attacked by prowlers, rolled along right behind us, his headlights on, blurring the magic of the night. Deep inside me, nevertheless, as we quietly moved on among the pines and the ancient stones, I vaguely agreed with the Count. I'd have needed to be alone and walk along silently, keeping pace with the extraordinarily peaceful and solemn rhythm of the countryside where, beyond nearly pale shadows, the bluish lightness of the hills was hovering. I'd have needed to stop alone in front of that little lady who has been standing there speechless in the high grass, keeping her hand shyly over her heart, ever since the time of the Consuls when she'd placed that hand, for the last time, over her beating heart, drawing the folds of her veil across it until death changed her into a statue and time made her sink imperceptibly into grass through which the wind of Rome has never stopped blowing.

Vesperal

Baedeker's, that extremely serious travel guide, recommends going up to the Janiculum Hill in the evening, at sunset. The Romans, who have not read it, do so instinctively. We thus don't feel so ridiculous when we follow its advice. But Tasso's oak tree ('All'ombra di questa quercia, Torquato Tasso, Vicino ai sospirati allori e alla morte, Ripensava silenzioso Le Miserie sue tutte'*) retains us less than the nearby small anonymous theatre which, in the shade of a few

---

* Returning to this spot years later, after having read Goethe's play and translated a few excerpts of *Jerusalem Delivered*, I'll no longer have that juvenile disdain for culture; and imagining that the lightning-struck tree, that ruin of a tree, could be the same oak tree that offered its shade to the melancholy marvel-maker of Sorrento when he had to take refuge in the Convent of Sant'Onofrio, will no longer seem to alter my relationship with the Rome of today but, rather, to enhance it; as if the memory of his words had its place here, around me, at least as much as the burning hot gusts of air rising from the din in the lower quarters, or the thick fragrance emanating from who knows what dark plant among the marble ruins.

yew trees, sets out its rows of brick tiers across from the yellow terraces of the city. We dreamt of organizing some nocturnal feast in this place open to aerial splendours; lovers were the only occupants for the time being, and entirely inattentive to the spectacle.

What is surprising in Rome is a heroic bad taste that surges forth more or less everywhere without managing to mar the most beautiful places. While the vast lawns of the Villa Dora Pamphili were turning gold on the sunset side and while, to our left, the whole city seemed ready to ascend into the sky, borne up and away by its glistening domes, we were examining the conquering profiles of the marble Garibaldians surrounding the flowerbeds, ignoring the obscene whiteness of the Manfredi Lighthouse (donated by Italian immigrants in Argentina) and, on the square, the martial equestrian statue of the hero. But there also was, among the trees, the 'poet's house' (who christened it thus, I cannot remember, probably our lyrical friend), where on another occasion I saw a white ghost leaning out of the window and where the three of us would have liked to live. Children were playing on the square where policemen remained mounted on admirable horses; on the nearby lawn, families were picnicking; a young priest pulling a cart had come to get water from a fountain perhaps sanctified by a monk who ended up as the pope.

The sun had gone down, but its yellow light and the day's heat were lingering as we walked down to

Trastevere. Between orange- or red-ochre houses whose walls were covered with delicately imperative inscriptions and, at the bottom, with a sea of garbage, narrow, winding little streets were swarming with squalling half-naked children, dark brooding girls and matronly women with undone hair; dogs and cats were prowling among the children. Sometimes, a horse came out of a small inner courtyard full of manure and hens; in the narrowest passages, the stalls of the *borsa nera*, lightweight stands of bread, fruit, cigarettes, and tables covered with a jumble of useful little objects—combs, wallets, razor blades— congested the street through which a barouche sometimes struggled its way through, not without creating an uproar. Withered garlands and faded bouquets suspended as votive offerings beneath the niches of Madonnas recalled that it was the day after a religious holiday. Often, in these impoverished quarters, a room opens directly onto the sidewalk; it is a kind of ill-lit garage in which lives an entire family who, at this hour, has invaded the sidewalk: the mother slouching in a chair, the children here or there, in fact everywhere, pissing, playing, squabbling, bragging. On Santa Maria Square, in Trastevere, well-off people have dinner on the terraces outside first-rate restaurants while horses slowly amble by, while a ball tossed by kids flies as high as the spray in the fountain and while, from the blazing shouts in the deepening shadows, the first star surges forth like a spark, all of a sudden hollowing out, around the campanile from which the bells are going wild, a sky whose silky coolness one would suddenly like to drape over shoulders that aren't there.

Scene

Behind the house there's a small terrace beneath a vine arbour, from which three stone steps lead down into a garden enclosed by a wall on which various things seem to have been painted. It's night. We pull the old sofa against the kitchen wall, bring over a wine flask and glasses. The weather is mild. Draped in a pale blue blanket, the boy is dancing with a silver-coloured bike in front of the fig trees; then Constanza, also slender like a boy, her legs bare, her face angular, her eyes sparkling below her blonde hair, dances in turn under the leaves; a gramophone is playing some music. The shepherd chases after the shepherdess, the girl provokes the boy, they're dancing, she's too nimble, he won't be able to catch her, they no longer want to stop dancing and the little kids of the house* wake up because of the music: 'Guarda, guarda!' When they lean out of the window, they're scolded, the shepherd and the shepherdess are whirling like crazed people,

* The house of the artist Giuseppe Capogrossi, who would later acquire some renown because of his attractive assemblages of usually fork-shaped hieroglyphs.

the kitchen lamp is casting some dim light on them, they're already in love behind their pallid masks and, at last, they collapse, breathless, laughing in their messed-up costumes, happy as if from a secret kiss. The little girl at the window has fallen asleep.

Monte Mario

Lélo Fiaux in memoriam

First of all, the suburb and the suburban fair; the city, on this side, abruptly ends with large tenant buildings, beyond which immediately extend messy fields, with shacks, at the foot of Monte Mario. But on the edge of these fields a little funfair has been set up: stands, merry-go-rounds and other attractions, the roller-coaster, lots of shouting and music. How could I have mentioned the roller-coaster in such a detached fashion? That evening, we never wearied of going back to it, time and again, and screaming wildly with each descent; when we'd arrive at the top—ah!—I'd prefer recovering just the view that we then had, down below, of the funfair which had started to turn on its lamps, of the humble fields, and of Monte Mario whose pine trees stood out against the golden sky! I remember stopping more than once as we were climbing it, up trails barely cut through ground covered with wild dusty bushes, to gaze down at

Rome which, as we hiked ever higher, became vaster; we sought to identify familiar churches, squares, even the roof of 'our' house. Down below, the din of the funfair continued apace. A family who lived there on the hillside, in a hut, with a whole tribe of children in rags who ate out of bowls like dogs, hardly paid attention to us. Eventually, at nightfall, we returned to the road that led up to the Observatory. The mild air seemed balmy after the sweltering heat of the Roman days.

I recall those black wooden tables under the trees; perhaps a fig tree stood nearby. A lamp turning the trattoria wall bright white was barely casting light on the family—two young couples and their parents—who was eating next to us; the red wine was gleaming darkly in big glasses never empty for long. We were leaning on a rather wobbly barrier, fashioned from logs, from which Rome could be seen sinking into the shadows until, all at once, its constellations were turned on. One of the opulent young women was cuddling up against her husband while laughing shrilly and lifting her shiny glass at the end of a naked arm vaguely outlined by the lamplight. We were speaking quietly, in hushed tones, and what we were saying was much less important than the shadow and the voices of those women, with their masses of undone hair beneath the low foliage.

Fregene

The grand plan to leave Rome and 'see the sea' had preoccupied their minds ever since the beginning of the stay. Thanks to Françoise's car, the plan could at last be carried out; it was the end of September. The beach is rather far from Rome, to the southwest; since we wanted to avoid Ostia, reputed to be so ugly, we sped (the driver had raced cars for Alfa Romeo) across large, nearly deserted, rose-coloured plains, then through a high, vast, pine forest beyond which a dazzling white fire was burning. They didn't initially grasp that this was the sea, 'their' sea, of which they had dreamt so often, and they were, without admitting it, a little disappointed. Several kilometres long, the beach was already almost empty; the cabins, shops and bars were closed. A group of children was still playing in the sand around a blood-red-coloured boat. They hurriedly took off their clothes and immediately dove in, their screaming and laughing almost seeming to make no noise in the big empty space. Françoise and Count Giacinto* were quarrelling. He was afraid of

---

* This Count Hyacinth, who has twice lent his illustriousness to these pages, isn't a mythical figure (though, come to think of it . . .): he's none other than the recently deceased composer Giacinto Scelsi, a friend of Jouve's and Michaux's; hardly less recently, radio interviews have revealed his humour, subtlety and quirkiness whereas a few concerts and recordings have brought forth his no-less-singular musical *oeuvre*. Some people consider him a genius; others, I'm told, a charlatan. I'm neither informed

mines (the war, indeed, was not so far in the past) and refused to let her go swimming, still sick as she was, so late in the season; they were shouting themselves hoarse, and it was rather ridiculous. Skinny, clumsy Mario began running along the shore just where the water licks the sand, for the joy of breathing in the sunlit salty air; his long limbs could be seen moving along in profile, like an ungainly wading bird. Marina had stretched out, naked, near the reeds; today, I think that she must have found her boyfriend to be rather indifferent. We could spot a greyish fishing village in the distance. Mario had stopped running; he was walking along in the fading sunlight, and the movement of the waves, which seemingly kept coming in and sprawling at his feet, made him sink into a kind of happy drowsiness. Just then, screams could be heard coming from the boats; the swimmers suddenly appeared to be caught up in a strange frenzy, and they ran over. A woman came up to them, screaming: 'Gino! Mio Gino!' Near the red boat, a very small boy was lying there, naked, a towel over his face. He must have ventured out too far. Nothing more could be done.

nor knowledgeable enough to judge. What is sure is that resorting to Oriental philosophy and mysticism, in our Western arts and lifestyles, although quite trendy, is rarely carried out deeply enough to be legitimate.

Venice, the first time

Upon our departure from Rome, the trip already looked taxing; there was no way of hoping to find a seat. We changed trains in Bologna and it got worse; no sooner had soldiers crowded into the aisles than they started speaking loudly and brandishing wine flasks without much consideration for their neighbours, and the train left through heat as hot as quicklime; we crossed interminable, monotonous plains without paying much attention to them, their richness seeming sad beneath the excessive sunlight. Meanwhile, it took an office worker several hours, and a whole sack of grapes, to overcome the resistance of a young woman to whom he was coming on strong: the scene took place without a smile; she kept repeating that it wasn't leading anywhere, that it was always the same old song, that she didn't believe him; but what seemed to bother her the most was the heat and those moist hands that were relentlessly trying to caress her. She gave in at the end. Fatigue had little by little overwhelmed everyone.

Towards evening, we begin to notice thin campaniles in the distance; we're drawn from our lethargy by an impatience nourished by many books and tales. With every new campanile, we imagine that we're reaching our goal. There's no question, of course, of asking our nearby fellow passenger who, moreover, is perfectly placid. 'Venezia Mestre!' Factories in the middle of the plain, a lifeless train station under the oppressive sun . . . Is this it? We don't understand anything. And suddenly a little girl in the next compartment cries out: 'Mare! Mare!' Indeed, we're at the sea. Outside every carriage door, the glistening water rocks and dazzles us as it fades into haze at the horizon! Sails are flying over it like seagulls; this tongue of the earth is just wide enough for the railroad and the road, which is why it seems we're sailing; and when we lean out the door window (although we've known ever since childhood, at least in Helvetia, that 'è pericoloso sporgersi'), Venice is already floating between the water and the haze like a light-grey squadron or an island glimpsed in the depths of a dream.

The station is a station like all other stations; we're lugging our enormous suitcases; but already the water of the Canal is shimmering at our feet. The curtain has been raised: all the palaces of this unimaginable theatre are in position, all the lace and glasswork whose rips and rust we can't yet see; we're so dazzled that, taking the landing stage bobbing beneath our feet for a vaporetto, we stand there patiently awaiting its departure. The end of day has already come; and nothing will have touched me more, as I crossed through the city for the first time to the lapping of the stagnant waters, than the big chandeliers coming on every now and then inside the noble storey of palaces whose fronts were darkening proportionately.

Later, beneath the beating bludgeon of the heat and also probably because I'd just translated *Death in Venice*, I became ill and my affliction lasted one night and one day; a night during which I had the time to detail every hawker's shout, every measure played on an accordion, every word and every footstep on the quay in front of the hotel, and then the endless lapping of the water after everyone had gone home; and one additional day that seemed to last even longer as I reeled through the stifling streets, cursing this unhealthy town full of artificiality, fabricated to delude stupid couples dulled by their conventional love and determined, having paid the price, to go into ecstasy about everything! Poor new Aschenbach who was going to die in a barbershop (which, I'm quite sure, I'd entered imprudently) without having had the time to get old, to know the glory that his model had experienced, without even the slightest beginning of a passion, whatever the kind! Moreover, palaces, domes, passers-by, fruit, canals and gondolas were already becoming ghosts to his eyes; he was already staggering among the shades, and his anxiety alone was real!

The power of literature bolstered by the sirocco! When my fever fell, for I'd really had a little fever— but the chambermaids had tenderly saved me—it was time to leave. Never had the city, and especially its less luxurious quarters which extended to the north and through which I wandered one last time, seemed so beautiful: a beauty of glass and haze enveloping me in sadness, but a sadness at last possessing the accent and sweetness of love.

Stopover in Genoa

After long, narrow, lilac-coloured fields, after arid hills and valleys, after one last train station immersed in the already fallen night, the town is announced by large, barely lit, apartment buildings. I vainly search for what I'd daydreamt of during the trip: a cool dark expanse that would be the sea. The station looks out on a circular piazza that is noisy, likewise poorly lit and surrounded by hotels and bars. Ever crippled with shyness, I enter the most modest one, trying to go unnoticed; there are chipped mirrors and dirty marble tables; a girl is sitting in a corner, her feet propped up on a chair in such a way that her naked thighs are mostly visible; she has the massive, ruminant-like head. A moustachioed young man is staring at her and smiling vacuously. I'm given little hope of finding a room. I've nonetheless set out to find one, with my suitcase in hand and a green canvas rucksack that must have made me look even more like the country bumpkin than I actually am. In front of me, nearly empty avenues opened out and seemed, because of my weariness from the trip and the weight of my suitcase, but dark gloom and solitude. Someone finally gave me the address of a first-floor boarding house and a taxi drove me there. The boarding house was located in one of those wide streets lined with high, rather dismal, nineteenth-century apartment buildings. I don't want to invent anything, only recount the little that I remember. I took the lift, rang the doorbell. A middle-aged woman ushered me into a shadowy hallway at the back of which and facing me—I'd put down my suitcase but had probably kept my ruck-sack on my back—a glass double door opened for a moment onto a group of girls wearing nightshirts or white négligés; they seemed to be quite young, pretty, and they were laughing (for obvious reasons). The woman answered my request by saying that she had only 'matrimonial rooms' and conducted me back, without further ado, to the entrance.

Today, I'll have the honesty to admit that, back then, I was quite naive not to have immediately understood where I was; but also, that I long regretted not to have stayed—since I departed once again into the night, ever-more exhausted, and finally found refuge on a makeshift bed put up in a hotel bathroom. The brief appearance of those eager and mocking little ghosts will nonetheless remain engraved in me for-ever, even as will, gladly, those women the desire for whom sprinkles and colours our dreams.*

* The next year, chance had it that Mermod, after *Death in Venice* had pursued me as we have seen, asked me if I'd like to translate three 'studies' by Thomas Mann, one of which was devoted to Nietzsche. I experienced some astonishment, as well as a kind of

The next day, having met up with an Italian friend who was an actor and a stage designer, one Luzzati whom I've lost track of, I visited the town, which had still not recovered from the war. I remember huge piles of rubble, like slopes of fallen rocks, up which we climbed to gaze out from the top over that tiered chaos

pride, amid—to tell the truth—a rather undeserved feeling of connivance when I translated these lines: 'In 1865, Nietzsche, twenty-years old at the time, recounts an odd adventure to a fellow student, Paul Deussen, later to become a famous specialist of Sanskrit and the Vedantas. After leaving all alone for Cologne, the young man hired a guide who was supposed to show him the curiosities of the town. The afternoon goes by in this way and finally, towards evening, Nietzsche asks him for the address of a good restaurant. But the chap, who, to my mind, took on the role of a disturbing emissary, led him to a brothel. The young man, pure as a little girl—all mind, all erudition, pious and chaste— suddenly finds himself (so he says) surrounded by a half-dozen apparitions "in sequins and gauze" who consider him to be a waiting customer. Without glancing at them, the young musician, philosopher and devotee of Schopenhauer instinctively heads for a piano that he glimpses at the back of the diabolical salon, where he makes out (these are his own terms) "the only human being in the group who had a bit of a soul". He strikes one or two chords. The spell that had benumbed him thus being broken, he managed to make himself scarce.'

(But the gravest thing is to come: one year later, Nietzsche returns, willingly this time, to one of those places and contracts the first of the two infections that will be at the origin of the illness which, as Mann writes, 'is going to destroy, but also prodigiously exalt, his life, and in which an entire epoch will find its stimulants, good or bad.')

where the complete mass of ship-owners' palaces, with their studded or armour-plated doors, weighed down on the seedy little streets of the port.

We hung out for an entire night in the port of Genoa, not without my guide continuing to tell me how dangerous it was; either he was truly worried or he took pleasure in spicing up our expedition. I think that the harbour consisted of blackened walls so high that one could barely see a mast or a chimney above them, and even less a bit of the sea; but there were all those bars whose sign names each spoke of another country, another departure. I remember seeing Scandinavian sailors brawling in front of one of them; and, inside another, a dancing couple, that is, a huge, scarred, mulatto giant resolutely clinging to a pale and slender girl, still quite young, who had caught my fancy. Other giants, Blacks this time, seemed to guard the entrance to certain streets which were so narrow that three men could not go through them, side by side, and where signs illuminated by spindly coloured neon tubes dangled their garish words. There, as elsewhere, I simply went by, with not very widely open eyes, like an insufficiently real passer-by.

Two Notes

In this little port where the Temple of Venus has been dedicated to the Virgin and where fishing boats near the shore keep lit a garland of nearly motionless lights all night long, the evenings were ever mild. I'd remain on the terrace above the quay. Little would happen. Once, a little girl was kneeling next to a round creel in which she'd enclosed a kitten that she, laughing, was making go round in circles. I never weary of recalling her tender, rather mocking voice, which kept repeating, like a song, 'Mio amore!'

*

Up on the Prato di Sant'Agostino, from which the roofs of Sienna can be seen turning golden as the daylight diminishes, children play at the edges of puddles where dead leaves are already lying. Someone came over to the fountain; a mother called out; the shouts crossed the covered playground, school had begun again in September, and my own holiday was also coming to an end. But better than the too well-preserved streets, already almost outside of town, I especially liked the Fort of San Barbara with its towering walls at the base of which, when evening comes, boys play football with passion. The smallest children hunt for chestnuts under the trees which have suddenly aged. Then lovers go up to stroll along the rampart walk where the grass has grown, and from which one hears nothing but the intermittent noise of spray from a fountain whose existence, in these nearly deserted neighbourhoods, is astonishing.

Ricordo di Napoli

To Henri Gaberel

In Paris, I've always liked those 'passages' lined with little shops and often covered with a glass roof. Most of the time, the shops are old-fashioned and too modest to have changed their appearance very much since the nineteenth century; and seemingly only very old people, on the margins of modern life, can run them. Although they're usually perfectly honest music shops, perfume shops (Houbigant!), bookshops and haberdashers', the melancholy as well as the unvarying and somewhat-unreal half-light in which they're shrouded sometimes give them an almost suspicious look. A strong draft of dreaminess blows through these corridors of sorts, which seem fashioned to accommodate seers, fortune-tellers, cabinets of curiosities or the antechamber of a Turkish bath.

In Italy, the liking for the grandiose and the need to provide covered forums to town dwellers have provided the biggest cities, if not with such passages, then with the *galleria* which is a crossroads of passages. Of course, the often considerable height of the galleries (there's a poem by Ungaretti evoking the one in Milano), the noise permanently filling them and the superlative splendour of their numerous cafes remove from them the secret, seemingly ageless quality of the Parisian *passage*. This being said, the peculiar light given off by the tarnished glass roofs—a timeless, perpetually dull and dreary light—separates these places from the neighbouring streets and turns them into distinct milieus suitable for encounters more dubious than innocent, more disquieting than serene.

In any case, this was, probably not without reason, my very strong impression of Naples, the first time that I found myself captive of the town. That first time occurred just a few years after the end of the war; more than ever, poverty must have encouraged swindling, theft and all kinds of shady dealings in this city that had always had a bad reputation.

When I thought back on this later, the strange light hovering in the galleries much resembled, seemingly, that of the rooms of the Lausanne Natural Science Museum to which our teachers dragged us, when we were children, placing us among the naturalized wild animals, the geographical relief maps and the rock collections, as in a cemetery where nearly nothing could tear us away from our boredom. Yet in contrast to the lethargy of those cold, high-ceilinged rooms, it was here in this hothouse, in this aquarium, that black insects were constantly buzzing, a vague droning that intensified, at times, into rumbling beneath the glass-and-stone, bell-shaped lid that was chockfull of lyrical ornaments; and movements were likewise incessant, as if furtive, underhand, a dubious dillydallying of darkish human beings who, when seen from up close, appeared astonishingly small, shabby, as pale in complexion as dark in hair and eyes, and ever ready, like gloomy illusionists, to draw from their pockets the brief sparkle of a trinket when it was not black-market cigarettes or filthy wads of money at advantageous exchange rates.

One afternoon, when I found myself there with a friend while we were waiting for the departure of the boat to Palermo, and perhaps indeed in order to avoid the shifty looks and suspicious gatherings that all ended up appearing to be personally aimed at us, we took refuge, by pushing aside the curtain, dried-blood in colour, of a small variety show theatre. First, we had to go down stairs where mothers surrounded by the horde of their kids were begging; to disappear into cellars of sorts and then go up other steps, take iron footbridges, all the while guided through this dark maze by increasing noise. We finally perceive, through the doorless entrance to a theatre box, a cloud of smoke, a few rays of light, then a waiting crowd. Crowding into the box itself are matronly women, children and young people, some climbing up onto benches to see better; at last can be made out the scenery which shows (would one have guessed?) the bay of Naples turned purplish at nightfall but not to the extent that cannot also be spotted, indeed, a plumed Mount Vesuvius at the base of which a pot-bellied tenor is singing; his voice is capable of such suavity that it becomes, now and then, almost inaudible. A match flame reveals, for a second, an exceptionally beautiful face next to us.

Initially, it seemed impossible to associate the dark and almost larval world from which we'd come with these little revelries in the catacombs, this fragrant heat where the melody, drifting by with ease and in a kind of enchantment over velvet scales, from murmuring to uproar, made one think of an unending fireworks display falling back down in a shower of petals or honey on an ecstatic crowd. Later, I came to believe that the very excessiveness of poverty could find a balm in this excessiveness of mildness.

Many travellers, spoilt by the pure and austere layout of Florence or the warm harmony of Rome, have been disappointed by Naples. I loved it, actually, for being so remote from all kinds of conventional beauty, even if I also regretted that Nerval's Posillipo was nothing more today than a rental housing colony. I loved it for being violent in both sunlight and shadows as brutal as its din, with its yellow melons hanging from balconies of deteriorated buildings, its fishmonger's stalls worthy of Mantegna's most beautiful garlands (fruit, leaves and flowers); for being, unlike what we'd expected, the city of the crudest reality. Everything seems exhibited, displayed, proclaimed. So great is the poverty or carefreeness, or the combination of both, that people often have only a room opening onto the street; their life is like a shop window. I once noticed a whole family in bed in front of a television set (which, I believe, became rife there earlier than everywhere else); another time, a coffin placed for the funeral vigil between two thin candlesticks. I find such scenes neither beautiful nor picturesque. But like the noise, the crowds, the movement, the light, Naples has an intensity that ends up attaining a kind of grandeur. The sun boils the crowd in this deep, narrow vessel; nothing can do anything against this verve and vivacity; children run and shout among the most miserable ruins. Everything is exaggerated: the disorder of the streets, the baroqueness of the churches, all the contrasts. Above the old city rise vaguely Arabic, spun-sugar villas in the miserly shade of palm trees covered with dust as elsewhere, for mourning, heads are covered with ash.

POSTCARDS

To Michel and Loukie Rossier

To René and Maryse Lehmann

To turn one's back on the snow once again (and not only on the snow), to raise oneself up into the cold, like skiers, for the pleasure of descending towards that country that remains, despite the worst that history imposes and inflicts on it, the land of happiness, the land that helps one to recover bits of happiness; and it's true that once one pushes open the still-cold window of the mountain pass, it's already clearer outside, the light has imperceptibly softened. Our old bones that have nonetheless begun to grow weary, our eyes blemished with disillusions, our hearts mutely afraid of the future—all this frail and bizarre machinery has already, once again, started running better . . .

From the Aosta Valley (1)

At the bottom of steep slopes, thick fresh grass is bathing boulders that have seemingly tumbled down only recently. Upon them, in that grass and, indeed, on those boulders, rises a whole grid-work—like wobbly cages or gratings—fashioned out of very old grey wood that will hold up, near the end of summer, bunches of grapes that will still probably be tart. (It's odd that this moves me with every new trip into this valley: as something that is very old, poor, and worn down yet without being sad in the slightest, probably something that is elementary, immemorial, bearing a human patina at the base of these enormous mountains—as would ploughs and harrows.) Cages so old that they seem eternal, or in which imprisoned Time is singing a muffled song. Like those very old tools that astonishing human patience has lustred over the years. The cages shine a little like coins, barely so: like ash.

From the Aosta Valley (2)

The name of the little town? No sooner read than forgotten: our mount is galloping too fast towards its first treat of straw and hay!

But the front of the church was indeed orange, as if an eternal setting sun had been shining on it ever since dawn. Land of happiness, where even a church becomes a sunbathed piece of fruit.

Hardly the need to see it, even less so to say it; but it's like a lucky pennant that will henceforth flutter a little ahead of us, up on the left side, even if no State, big or small, has given us a 'mission'.

Or this: the colour of a physalis alkekengi, that strange flower that looks like a Japanese lantern (bad taste included).

From the Plain of the Po

Passing through the severe Customs Office of the mountains has been forgotten: they're now but wisps of fragrances, incense and veiled mirrors mounted on plinths of haze.

The pale yellow or russet (depending on their age, their variety?) poplars are rustling around the shiny meadows that they delimit, and the air is becoming iridescent.

These perpetually quivering leaves caught up in a light haze: is it really mere chance, or isn't it perhaps something being suggested to us in this way? If not. to respond to the leaves, then, at the very least, to glimpse this something (and it's like a puff of fresh air reviving us for a moment, a stream of leaves), while the other poplars—the real, more furtive ones—have also awakened everywhere, are also shining and multiplying the weightless March or April sunlight.

I'm surprised at myself for liking this plain better than nearly all the other landscapes of Italy that I remember.

Vast enclosures whose high barriers of trees do not close, even as it happens that words, instead of darkening the page, help to make something unknown awaken and, slowly, to take shape on it.

From the Plain of the Po, towards Bologna

The daylight has diminished, the sun is behind us. We feel a slight tiredness in which mirages of nourishment are becoming more specific: all the beauty of the world will not make sages or angels of us. Why aren't we alone in sliding down this celestial slope, why must there be noisy and dangerous commerce in every town, and how is it that so many foreign tourist boors are allowed to enter here? Is there someone who could appreciate, love this country as much as we do? (This initial tiredness thus gives rise to delirious ineptitudes.)

But, responding to the bare vine arbours of the Aosta Valley, here are the orchards of Emilia, some of which are already flowerless—knots of wood whose colour lies somewhere between brown, grey and rose and which will carry, hanging from their ropes, all the fruit of *The Georgics*. And on the right, something has been happening for some time now; the plain has been producing hills like a blue mist, even as a dream sometimes engenders an inaccessible sleeping woman: the Euganean Hills. The farms are pig-blood in colour and have the noble setting that sets palaces apart. Straw ingots pile up between their square pillars.

(With every chilly pre-spring, this was thus our overture as interpreted on mother-of-pearl flutes and gilded spinets, we being perhaps the only ones hearing them played so deftly, escorted by the whole invisible aerial orchestra in our employ.

First measures of silver, haze, and jade.)

Displays

Even on the motorways, inside those absurd bridge-
    stopovers,
ah!, those capital-letter Easter eggs laid by ostriches
    that Jupiter had seemingly made pregnant, eggs
    more pink or purple than is decent,
like, elsewhere, those warehouses of light fixtures
or those never fragile enough freaks birthed by
    Murano,
what horror for our shy refined minds,
    but what merriment!
Land of poverty and exuberance where we're paid
    with multicoloured pieces of candy,
where, beneath the cupola of Parma, Correggio lets
    go of all those baby angels, like balloons!
(Yet when he puts Danaë to bed one fine evening in
    a golden halo, like an extremely desirable cloud,
    then look at us all daydreaming, we poor lame
    brothers of Zeus . . .)

Crypts

Although we love those theatres where nothing ever seems crimson enough, golden enough, twirling and glowing enough to sweep us up to the sky with a whole squadron of cardinals, virgins, martyrs and angels, in a great hubbub reiterating at that higher level the commotion of the streets and the fruit markets, there's perhaps a better, in any case a more secret part of ourselves that leads us to the bottom of this short stairway even as one goes down steps, to a source, that are always a little moist. We who are farther and farther away from a source. There's little light, and this narrow space resembles a tomb; it sometimes houses them. On the stone columns a kind of flower can be made out, or less than that; the vaulted ceiling is low. But, indeed: it's like a very first movement upwards from the ground, and one could perhaps say that the ornamentation, the interlacing, are like an intensely purple flower trembling on a mountain slope. We're nearer the incomprehensible thing which, while still remaining closed to us today, secretly guides our footsteps, as those gems did for Novalis' miners in the womb of the earth. We come up against what is heaviest, hardest and most opaque in our world, on which, like a schoolchild on a slate, someone has seemingly begun a sentence that we've not finished.

From Mantua

In the immense maze of the Gonzagas,

has the woman guiding us on this cheerful grey day,
with her yellowish complexion and misshapen limbs,

come down from the frescoes of Mantegna? She'd fit
in marvellously. She's perhaps going to climb back up
into one tonight.

In the meantime, we're docilely following her.

From Ravenna

As one approaches this area, the commotion and
movement seem to decrease, the light to sink into the
sludge. The town seems farther from everywhere than
the roadmaps show. Imperceptibly, an inner distance
mists over it. We no longer need to hurry; to speak,
even less so. San Vitale is a brick hive full of the eternal honey of the gods.

From Ravenna, again

In this marble case, my remains have been reduced to
a few friable bones.

But the image of these two peacocks at my side is like
a balm.

Nowhere else have I seen greater peace.

From Venice

The Alps aren't very far away: a cold rainstorm is beating down like an immense flock of black birds on the bristling lagoon. Run for your life! Beginning with the drenched bride, exactly like Carpaccio's monks running off from Saint Jerome's nonetheless kindly lion.

From Venice, Palazzo Contarini dal Zaffo

The voluble Duke Élie is wearing green velvet slippers bearing his initials.

The duchess is sitting up very straight near the fire, a distant smile full of sweetness and discretion wandering over her face.

Then we go over to the table to eat.

It's as if we were entering a scintillating forest: for an instant, we reel within this green silvery incense as when we were children and the door solemnly opened onto the Christmas tree.

From La Fenice

We're under the arbour at that peaceful hour when the sun goes down; then the earth grows dark and a cool wind rises.

Unless this is a grotto whose walls are sparkling with shells and living flowers; and this same wind that has risen, a servant woman whom one would like to detain by grasping her hand and who is blowing out the candles one by one.

The chandelier is a ball of mistletoe: a Happy New Year to us all!

From the Fenice, once again

It seems that the century of court abbots isn't in the past. This pallid straight-backed one is guiding beneath the chandeliers a hirsute artist frightened by all this luxury.

Onstage, Verdi draws a hymn to life from a cruel story of Doges in which there's much bloodshed, as if he were transfiguring the commotion in the streets that has always muffled the worst acts of violence here.

From San Zaccaria

Every morning, I go to sit in the still-vacant church, in front of the same big painting. I no longer see anything but blue and green, as if of a sky and meadow. The gentle, solemn figures are so self-absorbed that they almost seem to be sleeping. Although they're holding no instrument, it's as if they had come together here to play a kind of music consisting only of infinitesimal variations of silence. This conversation, which isn't one, sketches around them an invisible circle that no disturbance can go across any more.

I'd willingly call this painting *The Source of Tranquillity*.

From Venice, towards Torcello

Everything—earth and sky—takes on a pearly sheen around a hermitage slowly giving way to trees and brambles. Black boats are ploughing along. Our little vaporetto, full of children armed with multicoloured glass sticks, is rowdier than a big aviary.

From Sienna

This fireman who nimbly climbs the ladder raised against a building, in the middle of the night, shatters a windowpane with a few hatchet blows, enters a dark room and no longer reappears from anywhere—nor does anyone else. Have we dreamt this up under the influence of those hard alcohols we don't deprive ourselves of?

Or was it Simone Martini who had painted the scene—some legendary miracle—for a predella? No one in the rather cold streets seemed to care about the matter.

From Rome

Ah, the power of words on one whose trade is to use them!

The Golden House! Nero!

Our group looks rather like a funeral procession led by an increasingly taciturn Hermes as we sink deeper into the humidity and the darkness: the burial of a small illusion . . .

Let's break off here where, without waiting any longer, a tireless faux-Brendel is playing his concerto of lasagne for us while the Coliseum, outside, as it has always done, keeps filtering the splendid midday light in its oval basin.

One last postcard, from Rome

This city looks like a great fire of embers smoulder-
ing in marble,

it's similar to an orange orchard, a mixture of fire
and night,

or to a vineyard whose grapes are harvested before
the triumph of the cold.

I put fruit in my cellar,

and when one goes down there, in winter, a candle
in hand, their fragrance, better even than a flickering flame, lights up the darkness.

The Baptism of Christ

I'd like to restrict myself to trying to define exactly, as for any other piece of writing, what I felt when facing that painting, in London, when, having just entered the National Gallery, my eye was still fresh; to define this feeling alone, however naive or insufficient this intention appears or is.

Now that I recall the experience, I know that I didn't think at the time of Christ who is, however, the centre of the painting; nor of the scene from the Gospels that is painted there; nor did I think for an instant that the three figures to the left, or at least one of them, were angels. And I asked myself not a single question about the figure taking off his shirt in the background, nor about the four bearded old men farther behind him. Something more general was surely acting on me, initially, wholly comparable to the first measures of a slow prelude by Bach; but also, to a portico of light-coloured marble columns, whose effect consists of a measure seeping into you, irresistibly, and not just any measure: a measure that is surely solemn, yet also joyful and essentially serene, that seemingly gives you, inwardly, the steady, peaceful pace of a procession. Indeed, so it was at first: an immediate restoration of order deep inside me, as I came to a halt. Also surely involved, subsequently or simultaneously (but, in this case, at a slight remove), was the presence of two groups of colours, like two flags, one of them in the background with dull colours befitting old men's clothes, the other in the foreground to the left, with bright clear colours confirming that some kind of ceremony was taking place; and the two crowned figures to the left, for whom I cannot determine, on the reproduction, whether they're in fact also angels (they seem, instead, to have come back from Antiquity or some other ceremony), have the round, rather hefty faces and almost placid look in their eyes of many figures depicted by this painter; and they must also have added to the serenity of the scene without my becoming aware of it, even as their luminous presence was also that of youth. But to retain me and leave me speechless with marvel, more than this had to be involved. It was, of course, that the scene was taking place beneath trees, even identifiable trees, and in the grass; that a hilly landscape gently rose in the background, with paths and towers, providing as a framework for the ceremony (which wasn't for me, at that moment, the baptism of Christ but, rather, a nameless, seemingly more ancient ceremony), the earth that we know, our home.

But still something else would mix with these elements, permeating them and playing a more mutely potent role: it was, naturally—and everyone has already seen it again in their memory—that clear sky where the clouds in their slightly shaded whiteness, far from appearing a threat for the azure, exalt it, make it deeper—as also does the dove, barely different from the clouds, above the lustral cup and the Christ's meditative face, and whiter than spring snow on the mountains, with its long horizontal wings—pure equilibrium; while by another miracle, at the bottom, where the feet are placed in a river so slack that it is no longer flowing, motionless like the rest of the painting in a suspense that is unlike something frozen, the sky is reflected, exactly as limpid and as fresh.

I then understood what was, moreover, hardly difficult to understand, that this great peaceful painting had retained me for such a long time in the strange, indeterminate space of a museum room, only because it was like a celebration of daybreak, of awakening, of the perpetual beginning of which water indeed washes us, whoever we are and however low we might have fallen, as long as it comes back at the end of night to surprise us.

Riva degli Schiavoni

I've gotten up a little before daybreak, perhaps awakened by the meshes of light moving and shining on
the ceiling like fishing nets, or by the horn of a boat;
or simply by the uneasiness sometimes born of
dreams. I haven't gone over to the window that looks
out on the open sea where the sunlight would perhaps
already be too scintillating; but, rather, towards the
window which, of the three storeys of this small hotel
with its decrepit front on which a name with gilded
letters is falling apart, looks out on the waterfront,
broken off nearly at my feet by a first marble bridge.
I then see before me what is by no means a dream or
a magic spell, yet impossible to translate, to transmit,
as one wishes: the still-deserted waterfront and the
uneven houses bordering it on the right trace out a
curve that ends, farther on, in a palace, while to the
left there's initially water and then, farther on, other
stones that are other houses, other palaces, one or
several churches; and I know that to the right, if I
went out and walked a little, I'd perceive, beyond a
wooden footbridge, the pink towers of the Arsenal
that hides, behind its crenellated walls, more gardens
than weapons (and it's already possible that at the
time this word 'arsenal', which had been laden for me,
for such a long time, with fateful mystery—ever since
my childhood when my first walks led me to places
surrounded by fields, outside the city limits of my

hometown and not far from a banally modern, green-and-grey camouflaged building also called the Arsenal—was already inseparable in my mind from Dante's verses which, moreover, are engraved in marble next to the entrance: 'Quale nell'arzanà de'Viniziani / bolle l'inverno la tenace pece / a rimpalmare i legni non sani'). But maybe that morning I didn't even think about it, and it wasn't necessary to do so; perhaps I only looked at those houses and those palaces on that paved waterfront, at the rocking motion of the anchored tugboats and the gondolas, farther on, and at the gliding of the first boats on the Canal; and it wasn't even this which mattered, but how to express this? Indeed, the words steal away, something like the inside of one of those shells that you bring back from a stroll on the beach, a conch that shows tints of pink, pale yellow, mauve, pearl grey, colours which are barely born and on which any word already bears down too heavily; and, especially, all this was floating below me almost silently; perhaps a little like the palm of a hand open for an offering; something which, however, was there, indubitably, yet like a rough sketch, a slow hatching of colours almost as imperceptible as a blend of fragrances; and at the same time, it was stone, and there were all of a sudden within this kind of tender kindling of a blaze, or in this rose garden (one ends up having to use such words), footsteps, not very noisy ones, to be sure, but, since they were the first ones, seemed more sonorous; there had been,

as if suspended in this ever-warmer iridescence, figures who had gone by, quickly, black like birds seen
against the sunlight as they're flying across the sky
and following a path just as straight, as if they knew
perfectly well where they were going in a city hesitant
to take shape. At such an hour, the footsteps were
probably those of still-drowsy workers or office
employees, perhaps shivering and little inclined to
marvel at the daybreak, who were hurrying towards
the places where they worked. Yet for me, intensely
watching all this from my window, not as a nabob who
would be forever preserved from all fatigue and anxiety about tomorrow but, rather, as someone to whom
had still been left the time and the energy to see, I was
intensely feeling there in front of me (or perhaps only
today, as I think back on it) the little that would have
been needed to enable these passers-by to be also
caught in this conch and raised by this palm, touched
by this wand made of the mother-of-pearl of this
dawn, so that they in turn would be coloured pink
and amber; just a little more fire illuminating the fronts
of the houses and I'd no longer harbour doubts about
the images that would envelop the passers-by, down
below, on the waterfront becoming less and less
unreal, images with the same tender colours as those
of dawn, but where it was Venus, just left behind by
the passers-by, who would be born again from the
conch, a mixture of amber and languorous ember.

*

Between these two dawns, between this fountain-like cool-
ness pure enough to ever enable the bird inside us to go
over any threshold and this reddish glow of embers which
is, rather, on half-opened lips, the final fire of a night
without restraint and without promise, I fear that I'm
unable to choose; and that I'll thus perhaps lose, like
Orpheus, because of looking back too long, the key to the
grand day.

Crystal and Smoke

The words 'Andalusian', 'Andalusia', how languorous they are, like looks from the black eyes of an olive-green face; how at once sonorous and tender, sonorous, clear and voluptuous like the word 'velour' (velvet); and their French equivalents 'Andalou' and 'Andalousie' rhyme with 'jaloux' (jealous) and 'jalousie' (jealousy, jalousie), that is, once again looks and windows, eyelids and slatted blinds, sunlight in white streets; which also links them, vaguely, to horses (for what is more horse-like than flamenco, the man rearing up, stamping his feet, the woman moving her croup and mane, that furious crackling in which ardour ceases not for a moment to be pride?) . . . One cannot know what, in the echo of these words, is due to the conventional imagery of this country, to the clichés of its 'poetry' which is, moreover, suspect because of the way tourism has contaminated it; be this as it may, something even today (nevertheless!) corresponds to the clichés. I hear pawing beyond the door that leads to these lands, and the rustling of silk:

I understand that daring and insolence, cavalcades and serenades, must have gotten along well, even as in Grenada snow can lie near orange trees—and all this, ultimately, is so Arabian, at least from what this layman can judge through a few readings of poems and tales from there.

*

What can be said, what can one dare to say when one travels too fast, always much too fast, as a foreigner without attachments, in this country? In any country? Yet I'm leaving such scruples at the door, once and for all, however legitimate they are. I accept the fact that, like any tourist, what I've seen—glimpsed—are mere images; and I'm conveying them as such, imagining that they bear meaning, all the same, and that gathering them isn't entirely vain.

*

First and foremost, that spring, those vast landscapes often seen below clouds which were so varied that the sky was seemingly drawing upon incredible resources of them without ever using them up, and which one day, between Grenada and Chimenea, became as black as ink or, rather, an almost terrifying soot colour as if spit out at us by one of those monsters who haunted Goya at the end of his life. And I think that what made those landscapes beautiful, besides their vastness and wildness (for the villages that one drives through, where one stops to have a cup of coffee or an anisette, still seem, in their whiteness, barely touched by time, sleepy, poor, perhaps overwhelmed by this kind of eternity and absence), was their foliage, abundant in some places, and their grasses born in soil that is dark ochre, russet or even purple, creating a sensation of grave, mute, intense warmth almost as if the earth were on fire, were made of embers—beneath the grass.

*

From my hotel room in Ronda (where I was of course moved that Rilke had made a stopover and, even more so, that the event had been commemorated, however ridiculously, by a statue), I could have contemplated for hours those fields over which was blowing a cold, violent wind and which one sees from higher up than the kestrels nesting in the sheer cliff. From that distance, the fields, because of their smallness and precise contours, appeared to be landscapes from illuminated manuscripts whose clear, impenetrable mystery they also possessed. The ground beneath the olive trees that was slowly being ploughed by an insect-sized tractor; the bouquets of still leafless trees near houses; the purple boulders amid the grasses of the slope that descended towards the stream; and especially that stream as dark and matt in the morning as glistening in the evening, that stream I'll refrain from comparing, like Lorca, to 'dense oxen' or, like Góngora who was probably his inspiration here, to a young bull, 'noble horns / its forehead ill lit by the moon', as if the word 'stream' alone should express its force, freshness, and sparkle—a lively current here, a lazy one over there in the fields, the link with the sky, the voluble response to an old childhood thirst . . .

The walls in the town were intensely white-washed and upon them was sometimes embedded, for the most noble houses, a pink or light-yellow stone ornament, an earth-coloured stone as superb as the tracks of an eagle's talons in snow.

*

And when our path crossed orange or lemon orchards—or when those trees were blooming in gardens, on the patios of palaces or churches—something again happened, I now realize, that was analogous to the impression produced by meadows; that is, the presence of fire amid coolness, of light within darkness; inasmuch as an orange is solar, the foliage of an orange tree seems close to night. Not to mention the truly suave fragrance of those little waxy flowers, an almost sickly sweetness by which we were incessantly led back, notably through the lively streets of Seville in accordance with the slope of our reverie, towards the church at the very moment when the censer is bobbing at the end of its little chain, enveloped in floating blue fumes, or towards the quarter where the palace women dwell, their galleried baths, their pavilions on the ramparts. And with this as well, I'm now amazed to see how it all ties together, how close it remains, rich in analogies which, however, would need to be backed up with more precise and solid proof.

*

One evening, while we were walking by, should we dip into a church to relax for a moment and take shelter from the commotion of the street (or from a sudden downpour), a vast, dark, and magnificently painted church such as the Monastery of San Jerome in Granada, nuns would be singing vespers rather out of key, in the silence of an almost empty nave, but their song, even clumsy and distorted, would be exuding an élan restoring life to those shadows—but I'm actually thinking of San Juan de Dios, which is right next door and was full of the faithful and not only old ladies as so often occurs in our churches— again we're facing fire, every altar is a gilded blaze, a glimmering of reflections as would also give off undone hair from which had not yet fallen its mother-of-pearl, amber or gold ornaments, we're surrounded by burning bushes—and surely as far from classical reason as from Protestant austerity—but be one irritated or not by this kind of crackling frenzy, at least it's as true; what it's tempting to call excess, bad taste or even blasphemy has its coherence and its language— and perhaps the rest of us, in our coldness, even need to submit ourselves to it, to yield, to let our eyes be irritated by sparks, to accept, at least for a moment, that nothing is ardent or rich enough, in the depths of nocturnal naves, for asserting a divine presence that will by no means allow itself to be reduced to a cold work plan.

*

And to head back from there and wander through the Arabian palaces and gardens, which are now mere empty shells (for we tourists congest them, but don't live in them), isn't to take such a long path when one is led by both the fragrance of orange trees and a matchmaker's voice in one of Cervantes' short stories.

Entering the rooms of the Alhambra, one has the sensation of having bee's eyes, so greatly does the ornamentation proliferate, teem and twinkle, yet not anarchically. One is in a cave with stalactites, under clusters of soap bubbles, big wasp's nests, one is in the lace and the shimmering of fountains multiplied by mirrors, and, indeed, one incessantly hears water flowing even down hollow stairway banisters, spurting up from basins, falling back down again—abundant cool water arriving straight from the mountains. This palace is comparatively less separated from its gardens which, more than surrounding it, blend with it. Everywhere there are openings without genuine doors; and galleries and pavilions where air circulates with the fragrance of flowers and the reflections of daylight.

Everything swarms in the coolness, and the glazed earthenware covering the walls seems more appropriate for enclosing fountains than for the walls of real rooms. One is surely more filled with wonder than moved while wandering through such places; but 'filled with wonder' in the literal and strongest sense of an expression matching the things that compel one to use it. This is, of course, the world of *The Thousand and One Nights*, a book much beloved ever since my childhood because of a few choice tales and its vivid imagery, a world that one discovers here in different ways than in a book, a world of subtle enchantment, of rustling, of murmuring, a world also of sweets and sorbets until one can eat them no more. For it's also true that one is at the limit of the too exquisite, the too precious, the too 'poetic' in these kinds of cages seemingly built for languorous birds. What perhaps saves the Alhambra from this danger is that the intricate yet ever-weightless splendour, the exquisite treasures, not without relation to the inside of the fruit that is the town emblem, are contained inside the severe reddish bark of the outer walls—and so close to harsh mountains which, during those days, blew all their end-of-winter chill into our faces.

*

A supreme refinement (not excluding cruelty—on the contrary), a kind of reinvention of Eden where the apple might well have been a juicy, burning orange, an architecture suspended above the smelly and noisy disorder of the lower town, even as a dream hovers halfway between the sky and the earth—a kind of aerial island, a boat full of lute players during a summer night . . . 'Don't give us any more!' one soon wishes to exclaim with annoyance, 'there are too many delights, too much sweetness, too much luxury, the time has come to break away from this languor!' Wonders, indeed, as we can easily see, like a complicated pearly shell found in the sand, a soap bubble that has miraculously remained intact throughout centuries nevertheless swept by all kinds of storms, yet uninhabitable for us, more remote than youth and even childhood, inaccessible even if, for a moment, we've seen it, drunk it down with our eyes, like a spoonful of rose-petal jam.

*

Unfortunately, I have only an incomplete knowledge of Spanish poetry; but I have no doubts that Lorca's is closely in keeping with my own few impressions of his country. Less gilded, less solar, less haughty than Góngora's, it's just as sonorous, yet a sonority like silver, cool and clear-cut like night. Here, darkness is never thick or murky; it knows no fog, no clouds, not even shadows. Steel and mother-of-pearl: the light is swift like a blade, cutting, cool like a torrent. Even tenderness is sharp, and languor, ardent. Things move

along quickly, clearly, like horses and trout. A guitar-
or harpsichord-like sonority, of course: curt, crackling,
sometimes aggressive. Everything can be found,
everything comes together: the soil of embers beneath
the grass, the little suns of the orange trees in their
night-like foliage, the fragrance of their flowers, the
altars ablaze, the flames of the whirling dresses, that
sky which, for the imagination of the Civil Guard,
'is nothing but a showcase of spurs', the water rushing
down from the heights of the Sierra Nevada like a
cavalcade. I sensed all this every now and then during
those few days, which still gleam amid the damage of
time:

> O city of gypsies
> who can forget you?
> City of musk and pain
> with your cinnamon towers.

(1978)

CRYSTAL AND SMOKE

Athens . . . a vast dusty labyrinth, a vast, noisy, whitish or grey aggregate of scaffoldings in the dust, above which one long seeks in vain the famous ruins, which appear rather too small from afar and still resemble rather too much what a thousand pictures have already featured. However, approaching the base of the citadel, one has the irresistibly strong feeling—distinct from any kind of thinking and even, I believe, from any kind of knowledge—that one is at the foot of a mountain. The Propylaea are the stairs of a mountain, and one's footsteps, even among a talkative procession of mostly distracted visitors, take on another dimension and another meaning. Up there, above the dust, one climbs into the mind. One reaches the floor of the gods. (And aren't those stair steps befitting Plato's feet the same stairs of the ascension that he imagines, in *Symposium*, towards the highest intelligible Beauty?)

A first sign, however, is given on the right by the Temple of Athena Nike: it's like a crystal, yet a crystal in which something like smoke, both blurred and akin to human grace, would show through; and more than once, while travelling, you'll remember this sign.

Higher up are those columns that become girls in a most natural way. One recalls the encounter of Ulysses and Nausicaa in *The Odyssey*: 'No, never have I seen a mortal, man or woman, like you; and in front of you, I feel full of reverence. I have never seen anything similar except at Delos, long ago, near Apollo's altar, the straight trunk of a young palm tree'. The gap of several centuries matters little: we're in the same world, one casting light on the other. It is a world in the morning. The pure water running across the sand or over the laundry washed by Alcinous' servant women has the same folds as these statues; Nausicaa's beauty is as upright, her smile as restrained, her nudity—by dint of being concealed— as fresh. ('The virgin, vivid, and lovely today.') Something begins in the crystal of this intense light, but it's not harsh. Perhaps nothing is more similar, than the Acropolis, to the sunrise as it takes place again every morning in that ancient era, in our dark times, or to the entrance of an upright, discreet and proud girl; whatever the hour, I say to myself, one climbs up there to see the dawn. And the korai of the museum, standing in a semicircle, are the morning hours on the face of a clock. Is it really a museum? Soon I saw neither the ceiling nor the walls. We'd been invited to the ball of the debutantes, with the difference that this was no 'high society' but, rather, the seashore, or the summit of a mountain; reserved, almost motionless, intact, with the colours of dawn already upon them, they were waiting for us; they were truly like turtle-doves, or doves, at once offered and inaccessible (and suddenly I recall Giacometti's girls also standing as if they were what remained of those virgins after a fire, but I need to forget them straightaway, those doves metamorphosed by some demon into crows), standing straight, their white complexions tainted with dawn, and I understand at least this, with my own body, with all that is inside it: that I have come here to receive the ablution of the dawn; a little higher than the dust and infinitely higher; so that it's also as if I were walking in the snow that will accompany us everywhere with its tender call in the diaphanous light, on its plinths of fog . . .

More motionless, surely, more silent, yet no less ingenuous than the few scattered seagulls on the stern, in the sparkling of the foam.

Perhaps, finally, like those islands that one makes out from the bridge, at night, surging forth noiselessly from the dark waves and also just born.

*

We've now come back to earth and stones by discovering, at the base of two harsh hills, a kind of cave, extinguished forge or fortress in ruins. Dandelion seeds are racing among the dry grasses on the domes of royal tombs. It seems that enormous boulders, fallen from some iron- and war-coloured planet, have embedded themselves in each other to build a den for bears, wolves or, even more so, lions whose likenesses in fact stand out, implacably, above the portal which remains standing and appears all the bigger in that one has to climb to reach it. It's as if one were going under their yoke, or under a haystack.

Lion-like beings must have lived here, and they were golden in colour; behind these boulders, in these mountains, they wore gold-leafed diadems, drank out of gold cups and handled heavy gold glaives; and gold masks with hard, narrow mouths and closed eyes were placed on the faces of the great corpses buried in a circle and guarded by high flagstones surrounding their tombs like the bordered corridor of a bullring. I'm little concerned by whatever historical and archaeological arguments might correct in this, but I couldn't see Mycenae without hearing Aeschylus' voice, the only voice violent enough to resound in such a place. Here, one is closer to the dark earth which like a crater gives off fumes of blood and carnal, animal passion. The watchman is squatting on the roof 'like a dog' (but at the same time he's preoccupied with the stars and with the fire, leaping from one hill to the next, that he awaits both as a release and a threat), the Erinyes who will lie in wait for Orestes are nothing but a pack of ferocious dogs, and when Cassandra screams out her vision of the murder, it's about the battle of a cow and a bull that she screams. Here, in the full sunlight of this May morning and the silence of this still-deserted place which, despite everything—one wonders how—is still remote, I cannot help but see spreading out, like blood flowing from a big royal body, the rug that Clytemnestra unrolls for Agamemnon's feet upon his return; cannot help but see her standing on the threshold, wearing her gold diadem and larger than nature; and cannot but subsequently hear the storm thundering that will ultimately reduce even these fortresses to ruins.

Footsteps become heavy here, stumble, and one breathlessly climbs the ramp struggling to tear itself from the dark underground; one progresses as if over the surface of a planet where gravity is several times stronger than on our earth. Blood stains the mountains; the missing door hinges creak when they turn in enormous anfractuosities; the gods are still lurking like caged beasts—and those of us who are wandering here, astonished, have hardly more substance than the slender shadows of flowers.

In the meantime, behind these heaped-up stones, this immense mass of still-bloody fallen rocks, appears a seemingly gentle valley at the end of which, in a grassy meadow, a tied-up black horse is turning in a circle. And on the path leading back down and passing further below, two donkeys peacefully approach, their burden of straw hanging, on both sides of the pack-saddle, all the way to the ground in a way that makes them look like African dancers in long reed skirts. Their hooves can hardly be heard striking the stony path in this vast landscape where two twin hills continue to rise, in the background, like two pyramids made out of rocks and brushwood, hills fit for no crown other than eagles soaring silently and out of sight. They cannot not be there in the impassive bright light, like the only angels imaginable in the sky, and they'll be replaced—once night has fallen, in an infinitely slower and more remote soaring—by the old constellations, the swords, the bows, the diadems of the immemorial night sky.

*

Epidaurus doubtless has the most beautiful theatre in the world and vast fields of ruins where hooded crows hobble about. But what moved me most of all was elsewhere, or, rather, merely anchored there in the ground by these ruins, and recalled by them as if by stones that seemed themselves to form handwriting along the ground, beneath the pines: as if the ample valley leading to the site were a calmly flowing river on whose green waters one were slowly borne along until one reached a hill-protected lake where one could do no more than let oneself be rocked on the bottom of an invisible, immaterial rowboat amid the imperceptible lapping of the plants, a supremely peaceful green lake—and we'd be healed of all our wounds, decanted, and would become clear like the sky, at least as long as the halt lasted.

*

Nafplio . . . It surely would at first appear difficult to speak about this town other than in a tourist-brochure-like style, to express what cannot be called anything but the 'charm' associated with more than one small Mediterranean port that is both lively and calm, old and new. But our pleasure must have had deeper reasons. First of all, I think this is because we arrived there by coming down from Mycenae, having glimpsed Tiryns in passing as a fortified island amid orange orchards and knowing that Epidaurus was nearby; thus—why not simply admit the fact?—we were electrified, as it were, exalted, with our eyes cleansed and wide open; and recovering the simple pleasure of living, after any real or figurative ascension, makes one marvel.

But above all, if I rack my memory, we could see blue mountains beyond the Gulf of Argolis and its bright waves tilled by the cool evening wind; as well as, further to the right, the plain of Argos which opens out onto the sea and, viewed from there, is like a genuine meadow, intensely green, with a few trees that can be made out in the distance; moreover, this green was truly emerald green, dense, precious, astonishingly so on the shore of a sea and especially of the Mediterranean; a green that was fully that of grass and plants but also something else that the word 'emerald' starts to express, without conveying it exactly, by suggesting an expensive ornament, an increased weight, a transparency and a force; a green of grass and also of water, an almost sacred colour—I obviously don't know how to put it, and many things in Greece will similarly exceed my means of expression—and one ultimately ends up thinking, once again, that light has much to do with all this as it touches things with its crystal wand and conjures up before our very eyes a real world closer than any other world to our secret dreams, when these dreams obviously seek to signify happiness at the heart of our darkness, when they offer to our bodies' sleeping rowboats, which are drifting and often about to capsize, this prodigious cape— which was able to make someone like A. E. (George Russell) imagine that he was thereby meeting up with past visions and, ceasing to be the nineteenth-century Irish poet who he was, participating in remote festivities with gods who at last had been recovered.

I don't think it's excessive to speak like this, even if, from another vantage point, the reality of a poor, long-oppressed, still-threatened country exists; even if every kind of darkness exists inside us, outside of us. Nothing will be able to extirpate this quality, which I'm trying to grasp and which strongly struck me although I was merely passing through like any other traveller, from these places where it haunts Seferis' poetry even as it haunted the ancient Greek poetry that already moved me at my school desk with, indeed, the penetrating force of a kind of light. Of course, one may object that all this has a mere physical meaning, that it's pure coincidence, a reverie and not much more. Nothing prevents it from closely matching the harmonizing power of our minds when they're at their highest point of tension and fecundity. I'm thinking again of the Temple of Athena Nike on the Acropolis. Something like a breathing crystal: am I being led to suppose that Greece is this, in the final reckoning (which is what I wouldn't be able to say of any other country that I have visited, not even of Spain or Italy)? This: emerald, yes, crystal, yes, marble obviously; yet into which would blend, like a shadow, like a wisp of smoke, a breath bringing them to life and making them lovable. 'For it will be made of pure light alone / Drawn from the holy hearth of primitive rays'. While passing by, we quenched our thirst with that light, we swallowed big misted-up glasses of it, and it produces the kind of inebriation that Hölderlin defines by means of a double adjective, *heilig-nüchtern*, 'holy-sober': the key to the mystery, perhaps, and not exhausting it. If Hölderlin had gone to Greece other than in his mind ('O Land of Homer!

/ By the scarlet cherry tree or when / The young peaches you sent to me / are turning green in the vineyard, / And the swallow is flying back from afar, telling tales, / Building her home in my walls, during / May days, while under the stars, / O Ionia, I think of you'), what confirmation his eyes would have received from that sky! Once again the korai stand in front of me, and they're not immaterial but alive and almost transparent. And the intense desire for this country in another poet who stands, in many respects, at quite a remove from Hölderlin and who likewise, as far as one knows, never visited Greece, inspired a rigorously and deeply apt vision for a few mutely and serenely melancholy poems where the specific word 'transparent' occurs several times: Osip Mandelstam. So that when I glimpsed from afar the summit of Mount Taygetus during a drive from Nauplio to Sparta via Tripoli, that mountain was not only inhabited, in my mind, by mythological memories, which were in fact rather vague, but also by the memory of that poet's lines in which bees and kisses blend tenderly: 'For all that's left for us is kisses / Fuzzy like little bees / Dying at the door of the hive. // They buzz around in the transparent thickets of the night, / Their homeland the dense forest of Mount Taygetus, / Their food: time, borage, mint . . . '

*

I'm indeed recalling that day in Sparta as it was experienced between the slopes of Mount Taygetus, with its dark forests from which a cold wind was violently blowing against us once we'd reached the summit of the hill of Mystras, and the plain—russet, green, golden, with its beautiful fruit orchards which, so it once again seems to me, are marvellously captured by Hölderlin's words when he dreams, in 'Patmos', that he's swept off towards Asia Minor 'where the garden, full of flowers, is ablaze, a calm fire'. Whereas the modern town of Sparta struck us as being a completely remote provincial small town, as far as possible from Helen and the swans of the Eurotas river, yet pleasant in the evening with its brightly lit coffeehouses on the main square, its strollers, its tavernas with their stained paper table-cloths and boisterous waiters.

It's enlightening to reread what Chateaubriand says about Mystras in his *Record of a Journey from Paris to Jerusalem*. In 1806 (the year when Hölderlin began to drift into insanity in Tubingen), he visited the town, already in ruins yet still partly inhabited despite the pillaging, and noticed 'Turkish houses painted red and green', 'bazaars, khans, and mosques', as well as men selling cuttlefish and sea polyps who looked like Franche-Comté peasants; he was welcomed by a Turkish notable, Ibrahim Bey, whose tenderness for his sick son surprised him in this place where ancient

Spartan mothers had shown themselves to be so harsh. But what is striking today is that this precursor of Romanticism and this adulator of Christianity who undertook his journey while thinking of *The Martyrs*, busy as he was to find the ruins of ancient Sparta in Mystras, has only disdain for the Byzantine churches and monasteries: 'Consider my embarrassment when, from the top of the Castle of Mystras, I kept hoping to recognize the city of Lycurgus in an absolutely modern town whose architecture offered only a confusing mixture of Oriental genres and Gothic, Greek, and Italian styles: not one poor little ancient ruin with which to console oneself amid all that.' His impatience will remain unappeased until he becomes aware of his mistake and finds the ruins of Lacedaemon a few kilometres away.

As for myself, who strolled all afternoon with our travelling companions along the steep slope of the hill where only a few nuns of the Pantanassa Monastery now live, I can only try to express once again, and it's not easy to do so, exactly what I felt.

Like almost everywhere else, we had go up to a ticket window and pay the entrance fee to visit Mystras. Now that I think back on this, I have the impression of having held out an obol to some mythological ferryman—just as soon forgotten—so much did it seem, as soon as we'd entered the enclosure, that we'd reached another world yet without having left the real one—in contrast to all those sites that tourism alters by developing them. We were walking on real earthen paths half-invaded by grass, beneath real trees, between meadows teeming with wildflowers; almost no one else was present, and the site is vast enough so that the rare visitors disturb neither its silence nor its authenticity. Forgotten the guard, the ticket window, the enclosure, the fact that we were tourists; it was as if we'd entered there by chance, having come from afar on foot, and were strolling along a mountain slope perhaps only to pick some flowers or to sleep in the high grass; and all of a sudden, a door opened in a very old wall, and on both sides of this door, an equally time-worn motif coiled upwards. The power of this stone ornament was genuinely that of a key that would have opened much more than a door for us. Beyond it, and attached to the cliff as if it had been born from a cave, was the first church that we'd discover in the shade of tall dark trees, the Peribleptos Monastery, where one has to stoop when going in and whose small, moist, dark interior, indeed like a cave, is entirely painted with Biblical scenes the themes or craftsmanship of which touched me less than the warm colour, however faded: a gentle fire that surrounded, enveloped and delighted us just as soon.

After which, we climbed from church to church rather like pilgrims going up the stations of the Cross, except that it was the opposite of a Calvary, a sort of spiritual ascension, as if we were climbing a scale of jubilant musical notes.

While heading up this way, at a bend in the path, between grey stone walls, we'd walked past a black-clad nun gripping the bridle of a donkey burdened with big baskets full of foodstuffs. From the gallery that gives access to the church of the Pantanassa Monastery and that is like a balcony looking over the golden plain, we regretfully looked away from the brick ornaments of the apse, which have the beauty of crafted rustic objects, and saw her arriving below us, in the narrow red-tiled passageway that separates the foundations of the church from the lower, bright-white dwelling that houses the nuns; two other sisters came out to help her unload the donkey; then they spoke for a moment about their flowers, their bushes which grew there in rose terracotta vases. All this, the words, the tranquillity of the animal, the white-ness of those walls, the faces of those women, exuded an almost supernatural appearance of peace; I say 'appearance', because I think that I later glimpsed in the eyes of a younger sister who was coming back from a walk with other nuns and who briefly glanced up at us, an unfathomable sadness which, if real, would be the only shadow staining the limpidity of those hours.

Why were we so moved by these churches which are scattered over the hillside among the wild grasses and whose ribbed-tile domes, like pieces of ripe fruit, Chateaubriand calls 'ignoble calottes'? I wonder if it's perhaps because of what distinguishes them from more open, more stunning Greek temples, that is, their closed-in-ness, their self-withdrawal, which makes them look like caves, or, even better, like attics (in which lies 'the grain of deep and perfect faith' of which Mandelstam speaks) or, still better because of their brickwork and warmth, like ovens for lime or bread that are suitable for protecting, for cocooning, for letting spiritual food rise or ripen; by means of their ultimately feminine, maternal quality to which we're perhaps, in the final reckoning, more sensitive, deep inside ourselves, than to the crystalline gleam of temples.

Pursuing the question further, I think that what engraved forever in my memory those few hours spent in the blue shade of Mount Taygetus is that, simply, mysteriously, in the shower, indeed the unmoving waterfall of the ever-intense light, those churches sunburnt by time, those enormous walls of deserted palaces or disarmed citadels, that Turkish fountain at the edge of a rising trail, in fact all those five- or six-century-old ruins are exactly as present, as substantial, and as unquestionable, with their weight of time and meaning, as the paths, the olive trees, the grasses and the prodigious variety of flowers, vividly coloured but predominantly purple, among which, one day, the churches will end up sinking. Byzantium was still burning in the here and now, and as richly and fragrantly in its own shadow as an orange orchard.

*

At the Thebes train-station buffet with its terrace pleasantly shaded by trees bearing clusters of mauve flowers and orange seeds, a kind of acacia that is widespread in Greece—a buffet which, for once, serves excellent grilled meat—the large inside room was almost empty at that late-afternoon hour: some uniformed men were merrily prolonging the end of their lunch, and an old, indeed ancient black-clad woman, probably the owner's mother, was showing neither bewilderment nor awkwardness whenever she answered the telephone. Because the museum refused to open for at least another hour, we didn't wait; but I found it hard to forget that this small, ordinary, sparsely populated town, dusty like so many other towns in Greece, had given birth to Pindar (the only inhabitant whose house was spared when Alexander razed the town), and that it had been 'Seven-Gated Thebes'; even as, on the vast yellow and green plain with its purple patches here and there, we were haunted by the ghost of Oedipus coming from Delphi, the same way we had come. That incredible din of destiny (whose echo still reverberates in our heads today), and now this drowsy little provincial town with nothing but the noise of backgammon games outside the coffeehouses.

I later noticed that Colonus, in those sacred woods an aged Oedipus found refuge—and it's as when a storm calms down and an infinite peace settles in below a more distant, gentler sky—was now a quarter of Athens just behind the beautiful pale- yellow, somehow Chinese, Peloponnesus Train Station onto which our hotel looked out.

*

Oedipus' shadow was still behind us along with the now-arid slopes of Mount Cithaeron where, indeed at Colonus, he dreams of hiding the bitterness of his old age, after having been taken there, as a child, to be killed; in front of us, there was Plataea, that is, the foundations of a great wall on which we could lean, in the company of a few shy goats—a wall tracing out, deep in the ground, the outline of a town; and a vast, slightly curved plain, completely calm and silent, at once vividly and lightly coloured, beyond which, at a great distance, I'm quite sure that the snows of Mount Parnassus could still be seen. I don't know if an archaeological dig has ever been made in these meadows and these fields—whose dominant colour, in my memory, is rather yellow, yellow-green, that is, warm, solar, heartening—and if weapons, bones and helmets have been found. For it's here, one year after Salamis, with Xerxes having returned to Persia, that his general, Mardonius, lost the battle that was supposed to end the Second Greco-Persian War. Today, we could have remained here for hours without moving, without doing anything, without saying a word, leaning against these ruins, in full sunlight, like seeds in the tepid palm of Demeter whose sacred terraces, not far from there, look out on factories and big rust-covered merchant boats.

*

I also should, in fact wish I could, speak about Delphi, about Andritsaina, that small town with its old, poor, wooden houses that already seemed very oriental to me, a town which, while we were eating cold pasta next to well-behaved schoolchildren who had placed their notebooks alongside their plates, was carrying out its daily routines: the chatting under the plane trees, the unloading of containers of wine (retsina or not); and especially about Hosios Loukas, whose warmish courtyards were rustling with grinning girls who were not, however, disturbing the nap of an Orthodox priest dressed in blue on his balcony; and about Aegina . . .

*

But nor will I manage to express properly what was grasped in passing: the dazzling harbour, the plateful of octopus accompanied by fresh wine under the awnings of a tavern, the cool shade as well—then the long bumpy ride in the bus, the orchards of pistachio trees with their light-coloured trunks, the dusty roads, the hermitages on a harsh hill slope, the slow climb unveiling the sea through the trees and, once again, at the summit of the island, that other temple dominating the last pines . . . Was it the most beautiful one? Something was happening there between the great solar heat and the brute force of the foundations and the limestone columns yellowed, almost scorched (one could say) by the sunlight: as if they alone were strong enough not to burst apart or waver in this fire, as if they were standing up to or, even, vibrating inside it. A kind of solar pipe organ, truly built for celebrating even today a perpetual victory, a calm and manly triumph. Among the crackling pines.

And to better understand what stops us short in such places, a perhaps useful indication is found in Hesiod, who comes only a century or two before Aegina and who writes about men greedy for money at the beginning of his poem *Works and Days*: 'Poor idiots! They don't know that half is worth more than the whole, nor how much wealth there is in mauves and asphodels.' When I read elsewhere, among his almanac-like advice for peasants—'But when the snail rises from the earth to climb trees, fleeing from the Pleiades, it's no longer the time to pickaxe the vineyards but, rather, to sharpen the sickles and waken your servants'—I understand that I'm still in an era when iron tools, animals, plants and the movements of constellations are linked by simple, strong bonds; and I tell myself that these temples, only the great ruins of which are still visible, were dwelling places reserved for the tying and re-tying of those bonds which are broken today, for our despair and, perhaps, our downfall. We wouldn't experience so much deference in front of their debris if they hadn't been endowed with deep meaning, if they hadn't accomplished an essential job of listening to and filtering the most distant messages, of transforming those sound waves into human speech. And I know well that radars can be found more or less everywhere today, gigantic concave ears probing the vibrations of the ancient ether, but the genuine voice perhaps hidden in the vastness is no longer heard, no longer translated, so that the most miraculously precise instruments, the most sensitive apparatuses, although they amaze us, often don't really seem necessary, nor truly fertile.

*

Necessary for what? One mustn't speak on false premises. One surely doesn't want to go back in time and pray or sacrifice in those temples. Nor daydream of some big expensive show that would revive them, as has become the too widespread habit. All those ancient buildings are vessels sinking slowly into the earth. For me, those temples can be only reminders fated to remain inevitably remote, the superb proofs of a possibility of harmony, thus a sort of way out that is repudiated by everything today but that interests me more than our sequences of negations, our clouds of black ink, our delectation over leftover scraps. I listen to another piece of advice from Hesiod: 'May your feet not cross the beautiful waves of eternal rivers before you have made a prayer, your eyes turned to their beautiful current, your hand first cleansed in the white lovely water.' To my mind, these words and the collapsed temples are linked. And the link is also a kind of light rather than a teaching.

*

Nowhere else in the world as much as in this country, during this trip, the still-habitable earth—plains, fields, valleys, seashores, and forests—appeared to me as akin to a song, and it seemed impossible that songs made of human words hadn't at least once been added to this song; a song akin to a continuous, steady, yet not monotonous song; a song that is profoundly a song all the while being constantly subjected to slight modulations that transport you from place to place, from halt to halt, in a sort of inner jubilation and harmony with the wholeness of everything that exists; and you're consequently ready to listen again in every site, even from afar, in the sacred enclosure, and while trembling, to a murmuring near-eternity that all these temples were not enough to encage.

*

And I'm going to be told, I'm already telling myself that all this is a little 'too beautiful', too foreign to daily life, to all the kinds of pains that end up vanquishing our weaknesses. Yet all this also exists, at least existed, and we travel a little to assure ourselves of the fact. Can we really no longer take part in it? Why is it that when we come back home we sense such a serious degradation, disaggregation? Why are we frightened to think that everything that delighted us in these trips lies in the past—except for the almost immutable landscape and encounters when frail human goodness still burns, all while seeming lost and like a uprooted flame?

The distance truly seems to grow constantly, mercilessly, between us and such joys; and it's probably for that reason that I haven't been able to speak about it as simply as I'd have wished. Nevertheless, this altitude exists and induces these perhaps premature, too facile flights, as one will say. The question raised remains the same: the relation between what is high and what is low, between vision and sight, grace and gravity. There are no angels on the pediments or on the friezes of Greek temples; few or no monsters as well; there are men whom I prefer not to call 'idealized', for that would be false, but rather surprised, captured in those moments when their lives, and our lives too, despite everything, are transfigured by who knows what insight coming from much farther than themselves; so that the inscription that they have therefore engraved on those ruins can still be read, in our day, as a reminder, an exhortation and a promise despite the worst.

(1978)

GLIMPSED IN EGYPT

To Henry and Suzanne

Cairo

More than any other moment in this enormous city of which I caught a mere glimpse, I'll remember our arrival, at twilight, when, on both sides of the road coming from the airport, appeared at the same time, to the left, the vast necropolis of the Mokattam, and, to the right, looming above us against the sunlight, the silhouette of the Mosque of Muhammad Ali. How to understand, and share, the emotion that then gripped us?

The time of the day probably had something to do with it. (In broad daylight, the magic would almost have completely faded away.) Twilight transfigures, renders all things less precise, harmonizes them like glaze in painting, increases their portion of strangeness. And this was Cairo, our first encounter with it. We knew we were passing alongside an immense cemetery, a city of the dead; and this city of the dead was almost blending with the hills against which it had been built because of its generally grey colour, tinted with ochre and rose, colours from which emerged, as if from a hazy lake, a few more venerable tombs and some small, purely shaped mosques; whereas the big mosque with its fake luxuriousness, to the right, which is merely a sort of Fourvière Hill when one looks closer, nonetheless imitates rather well its model, Saint Sophia, and as it looms against the sunlight, it thereby produces a prodigious exotic effect on an unprepared traveller naturally inclined to enthusiasm.

On the boulevard we were driving down, our century's haste was pushing its noisy, nauseating, seemingly blind waves one after another; all the same, this haste will have given us enough time to take in these signs, to the left and to the right: the immense necropolis where today's poverty brings the living and the dead together, and the ample cupolas, the high towers which, against the sky, continue to sketch shapes that speak of a god.

I still think back on that moment of twilight, vaguely, confusedly, as we experienced it, with its chimerical aspect. It was as if we'd suddenly come up alongside a vast camp of military tents above which had been raised a standard whose symbols were a cupola and a tower, a semicircle and a vertical line, against the dusty, golden backdrop of the twilight. Not much in common with the exuberant and agonizing reality of this town, but this matters little: we're also sometimes exposed to mirages and they aren't entirely void of meaning. This one made us meet up, for a moment, with what is expressed of Islam in the surahs of the Quran or an Arabic poem, like this fragment of Imru' al-Qais, reinvented by Armand Robin:

> I surged forth on a fast bay-brown horse, its body dried off from galloping across so much sand; a weaver's beam seemed to have slimmed down its hardened flanks.
>
> Both of us leapt, breaking through a terror-stricken herd of gazelles, their hides pure and with the hemmed striped fabrics of Yemen on their embroidered tibias!
>
> And as this flustered, panicked herd at Djamama scattered, they seemed to me and my horse to be a mirage of white-draped horses fleeing and veering every which way!

A world of stones, earth, and sand. Later we'd glimpse, ever while passing by, those little village cemeteries, along the roads, which were even more astonishing than the severe, moving seracs of the Jewish cemetery of Prague: those few rocks standing on their point in the sand, distinguishable from an ordinary rockslide on a mountain slope only because of their more blatant geometry. Down there, truly, with the torrid air at hardly higher levels and that eye-burning light, there's no place for rotting. No place for any hesitation, complication, for any detour, any regret! The reduction to bones, as to stones, and, if one can still believe it, radically, fiercely, to the invisible, is immediate, forever, as in the landscape outside.

*

On the sidewalk of one of those narrow streets through which even buses somehow slowly manage to edge their way, in front of a chaotic little shop of a kind abundant in these poor neighbourhoods, wealthy black-clad women decked out in cheap gilded jewellery and garishly coloured scarves have sat down for a while in big, probably wooden armchairs that have the most contorted imaginable shapes and have been painted so glossily white that one thinks of concentrated milk. An ugliness so straightforward and garish that it becomes merry and almost likeable.

El Haranyia, near Cairo
(or perhaps elsewhere, in the same area)

In one of those workshops where very young children are weaving rugs before our very eyes (and we wish the rugs were a little more beautiful so that we we'd really want to take them back home). The smiles, the looks in the eyes of the little girls (was the one who keep insisting that I sit next to her, at her loom, even ten years old?) have a grace, a vivaciousness, a fire that could melt the most hardened traveller; without one being able to spot the slightest ambiguity in those looks and smiles. (Really? One doesn't know what to say, if the same game goes on all day long . . .) But what sparkling, what merriment can be produced by the charcoal of those eyes!

And I don't distance myself all that much from those little she-devils when I think of what rather often humanizes Egyptian statuary: those princesses who are often represented as tiny figures along the legs of royal colossuses. Whereas we need to raise our eyes to make out the heads of the colossuses, which loom over us like a capital on a column, the little princesses are at eye level, also standing very straight; and also always almost absent, with vacant looks; but so much suppler and fleshier, all the same, that one wants to touch them, to thank them for being there, at the foot of their sovereign, instead of a whip or a sceptre.

Of all those graceful figures, the one we're least likely to forget is the goddess Nut, the goddess of the sky who is sculpted on the inner side of the lid of the sarcophagus of Psusennes; a pair of mirrors creates the illusion that she's lying at the bottom of her tomb: a long, slender, white, teenage body adorned with stars from head to feet.

The Shores of the Nile

With their masks of very ancient yet extraordinarily silent and placid warriors, the heavy ash-coloured buffalos have crushed the dry sugar-cane stalks that crack under your feet and prevent them from sinking into the mud. I saw there in the groves of reeds—while, on the other side of the river, seemingly floated the arid mountains where the great dead are buried, watched over and protected by the freshest colours of life—a kind of sand-coloured, absolutely motionless heron; and, hardly more lively, a hen called a 'sultan' probably because of its plumpness and beautiful blue plumage. In contrast, some black and white birds of the kingfisher family, the ceryles, were swirling like trapeze artists, inebriated with their own acrobatics, just above these reeds.

A little higher, along a path fitted out for strollers halfway up the slope, the Nile acacia has little necklaces of seeds that would not be unseemly for little girl pharaohs.

A great quietness reigns almost everywhere on these shores. As if the slow, silent movement of the river that begins so far from here in thunderclaps, resulted in this. Between two vast empty expanses,*

---

* And I recalled Góngora evoking, in the *First Solitude*, the Nile, that 'king of all rivers, on whose banks / the wind inherits vast / spaces by the barbarous tombs Egypt / erected for its pharaohs / long since vacated . . . '

two realms of dust that sometimes dispatch, at a gallop, their blinding banners of sand all the way to here. One day, we saw them passing by not too far away.

Seen from the boat

It's as if we were sitting in a cinema that was showing a documentary called *Landscapes along the Shores of the Nile*, except that we're spared the commentary and the musical accompaniment; except that there's no ceiling, that we breathe in the air of the excursion and it can be chilly, that we're free to move from this cinema to another one and even take a nap if the show becomes too monotonous. And we know that everything we're being shown is true, real, actually experienced. Harshly experienced, perhaps, when one thinks of it; and since you happen to imagine it, it also happens that you feel ill at ease. But in that case, in order to straighten out one's position with respect to one's conscience, one would need to give up travelling, especially in poor countries. It's indeed not possible to go further into this, at least for now—or a completely different kind of approach would be necessary—so as not to spoil our wonder, for we're grateful, like so many others before us, that what we're seeing is admirable.

But I'm not sure that I can say anything better than the first tourist brochure at hand. Everyone has specifically noticed that the scenes spotted from the boat have something 'Biblical' about them; indeed, according to all appearances, neither the landscape, nor the few houses between the trees, nor, even more rarely, the clothes of the people, nor their kinds of work, have changed markedly over the centuries. As I was often watching the shores through binoculars, which focus on and, since they focus on, intensify the scenes, it seemed to me, more than once, that I'd isolated a detail of a Renaissance painting, one of those fragments of landscapes that one always discovers with pleasure in the background; and once, more precisely, a detail from Poussin's *Summer*, at least as far as I remembered it. Once I'd verified the comparison, it appeared less rigorously grounded, but it deeply touches upon something that is true. The impression indeed depends on the permanence of gestures and costumes; even more so, on the equilibrium of the few colours—green, yellow, brown, ochre, blue—among which stand out the more vivid hues of a dress or a turban; on the harmony of lines, as well as on a great apparent tranquillity created both by the predominance of the horizontal and by the sentiment of near-immutability inspired by the permanence of the costumes. One comes to believe that, alongside the eternity imposed upon the mind by the dark, enormous majesty of the granite monuments, this more affable, more vibrant kind of eternity subsisted on the narrow margin remaining, on each side of the river, to the life of the Egyptians. This is how we thought we'd seen, for a moment, the Three Wise Men walking in procession among the sugarcane fields, or Rebecca stopping once again near a well.

Once we come across them in groves beneath their true sky, the palm trees which are so pretentious, ridiculous or filthy, when they're exiled to the parks or wharfs of our southern towns, have a very special kind of nobility, very different, for example, from that of an oak tree; closer to geometry, they're also closer to ornaments such as are lavished on palaces: wide fans, panaches, big crowns, yet they're also extremely supple, docile to the slightest puffs of wind, and perfectly at home in a classical landscape where, as in Poussin, nature matches up so well with monuments. And the intense foliage truly shines like an emerald against the sandy background.

As we come back down the valley, this time by the road, and discover villages made of dried mud, propped up against the first foothills of the desert— and as if we were discovering in this manner the harsh backside of the eclogue—what should we think about the lives and destinies of those Egyptians whom we catch unawares in their daily life, irrigating a field, cutting plants, sometimes praying while turning towards an invisible Mecca, crouching and drowsing near a water pool or riding on the back of a donkey? We tell ourselves that they're used to this sun that would appear so quickly implacable to us, that they're used to the dust and stones that have always been their lot; that even if they're very poor, they're protected, by means of the unchanging slowness of their days, from the frenzy gnawing away at many of us who have all we need. But this means reassuring oneself too easily. So I'll add nothing to a theme about which I know all too well how much illusion lies in store for us. Avowing willingly that I've seen only images during these few days; but among the most tranquilly beautiful images that can be gathered in this way, from too far away.

Esna

Today, what remains of the temple dedicated to the ram-headed god Khnum, the potter who created the world, is merely a large, very dark, lavishly decorated hypostyle room at the bottom of a hole; since all the openings have been fenced off with wire mesh, probably to keep birds from nesting inside, it looks like an empty aviary from which, on the contrary, all the immemorial souls of the dead have fled to avoid getting mouldy. Looming over it, on one side, is a tall, very old house with its finely carved wooden loggia, rows of earthenware vases designed to maintain a cool temperature, and with a threatening crack running from top to bottom. An old woman, however, is still standing at one of the few windows. Our wives are advised to avoid the backrooms of the sometimes too over-attentive shop owners. The children waiting for us on the riverbanks, hoping to sell us filthy ragdolls, seem especially wretched here. All of a sudden, we're very far from the eternity of the gods, from the magic that should have helped us to reach them and, even more so, from all kinds of idylls.

From the onset, the mere word 'Egypt', like that of 'Tibet', has been connected in my mind to a vague yet strong feeling of sacredness. The word loomed somewhere, faraway in space and time, like a sphinx defending the most solemn mysteries, those of the Beyond, those of death. Such was and still is the case for many minds; and it's no matter of chance if the 'Landscape of Laments' explored by Rilke in the last *Duino Elegy*, as if to give the sequence its genuine orientation, resembles an internalized Egypt.

When I was young, I was fascinated by anything that touched upon the sacred. I see myself once again, just after arriving in Paris—while sitting in the peaceful, reassuring, greenish light of the Bibliothèque Nationale—leafing through old Mesopotamian rituals the dust of which, so I wonder today, I must have forced myself to shake off; not without thinking that the young man who I was back then would have had better things to do than to compare the Egyptian *Book of the Dead* and the *Bardo Thödol*.

*

My exchanges with Gustave Roud, which mattered so much to me during my early adult years, encouraged me in the same direction. Using a German version, he'd translated a few Egyptian poems about death. When he was an old man, those ancient words had remained closer to him than anything else. And the present that he gave me, in 1950, of an invaluable book about the Cairo Museum—to thank me for a homage that I'd organized in his honour—clearly shows that he thus knew, thoughtful as he always was, how to make me especially happy.

Later, nothing came to deepen or specify the meaning that this word, and this world, could have in my mind; this is because I've never tended to deepen anything.

More than forty years thus went by before an old and generous friendship enabled me to see on the spot, in an almost unchanged landscape, the monuments that have subsisted from this remote civilization.

*

What I first noticed during this trip (besides the joys of friendship) is that at no moment, or almost, did I feel the stupor for which ancient Greece had a name, *thambos*, the frisson that gripped me, indeed in Greece, more than once during the two trips that I took there not so long ago; for instance, at the base of the theatre at Epidaurus, or at Mycenae, or while walking up to the Acropolis; more than at Delphi or on Delos, as opposed to Heidegger (if I may be excused for the comparison!) who found only on this small island the equivalent of what Hölderlin (or, through him, Sophocles or Pindar) had made him sense of the essence of Greekness . . . This doesn't mean—or I'd have to be pitied—that I wasn't surprised, spellbound more than once, and filled with admiration in front of the monuments of Egypt; but in these emotions, something was missing all the same: a trifle, almost a trifle. It was important for me to find the reason or the reasons.

*

Nothing obviously rules out that this depends on me alone; this damned wearing down of the heart, of the body, of the mind against which, even if one resists, little can be done. And circumstances that everyone knows and deplores might also have been involved: the crowds, omnipresent on tourist sites, who don't have the legitimacy of those who brought to life these still-lively places to celebrate feasts; the impossibility of completely isolating oneself from the crowds and, even more so, of returning to the sites, of freely lingering there, of wandering aimlessly at various times of the day as ancient travellers were able to do. However, it seemed to me that the real reason was more meaningful than this and that my mind was less worn down than had changed in regard to those youthful years when I admired an art, more than any other art, of which, now that I think of it, I knew and understood little.

*

In an *Encyclopédia Universalis* article, the Egyptologist Claire Lalouette observes that Egyptian art monuments ultimately form nothing but 'an immense magical apparatus of resurrection'. When I was there, nothing seemed more exact; and this was the essential fact. At all costs, the pharaoh (and, consequently, those around him) had to be given the ability to accede to the eternity that is the privilege of the gods. In eternity, the gods move as bright immutable stars seem to do. Only a religion to this extent obsessed with eternity could impose a similar constancy on its visible forms, those of temples and the bas-reliefs that adorn them, and those of rituals as well. An inexperienced eye cannot immediately distinguish whether such-and-such a ritual scene represented on temple walls dates to 2000 or to 200 BCE.

Of course, Christian art has unflaggingly taken up the same scenes; but their representations have changed rather profoundly from century to century, as have the shapes of churches. Egypt will have imposed on time its obsession with eternity for nearly three millennia.

*

In the world of eternity, to which only magic can give access, the gods have no faces; only masks. The same is true, in art, of the pharaohs who must identify with them (except during Akhenaton's brief, strange, moving interlude). May one surmise that the face appears with history, with the dramatic taking into account of time?

*

Often, in front of those works, many of which are admirable, I thought again of the korai of the Acropolis Museum, of how they're just beginning to smile, and I said to myself: If you don't feel completely satisfied, then isn't this what you lack: The incarnation of gods?

*

Moreover, it's not insignificant that the religion of Egypt, for as long as it reigned over the country, remained sterile, as opposed to Buddhism and Islam; and that it survives, today, only to nourish the nostalgia of a few vague occultisms.

*

However, the Egyptian religion was remarkably consistent. Because it subordinated everything to eternity, why should it ever have modified anything in its ritual, its imagery, the forms of its architecture?

It will therefore not have experienced one of the difficulties of Christianity which has become cruelly visible today: If Christianity claims to assert an intangible truth and an eternal God, should it also have left untouched the forms that translate it in our world? How can he who refuses that the Latin Mass and the Gregorian chant be abandoned—and something in me approves of this because few other kinds of music, or so it seems to me, better translate eternity—accept the evolution of the forms of churches where such services are held? Yet supposing that he doesn't accept this, for which period of religious architecture would he reserve the privilege of being the only legitimate one? And once one cannot help but notice that temples that never change their form, as is the case in Egypt, sooner or later lose their meaning—exactly like literary forms—can one conceive, even for what must continue to represent eternity, something other than forms that change? Even if one maintains faith in something transcendent, can one imagine that no religion of this world escapes degradation and death?

*

In all likelihood, it was thus time's shadow that was missing for me on those too-impassive bas-reliefs and paintings, even when their hieratic quality possessed an economy of means, an elegance and a limpidity that were sovereign. Seemingly missing were the marks of history, of a story, an ordeal, a drama; a proximity.

During those few days in Egypt, I didn't only think of the korai of the Acropolis; because I'd just seen them, I was also persistently revisited by the figures of the Brancacci Chapel who are so noble, so pained yet calm in front of those rather arid beginnings of landscapes. Those men and women, young or old, in those beginnings of places recognizable even by us today (the mountains, the streets, the shores are already ours), although they still retain something of the majesty of columns, of the saintliness of officiating priests, have taken the first step outside of the eternal Garden; and because they suffer, because they know shame and regret, it's towards us that they're progressing. Such, I said to myself, was indeed the world—seriously wounded by time yet, in one sense, healed of time nonetheless—to which I still belonged; even if, with respect to this world, the distance also increases a little more every day.

*

But at Olympia, at the entrance to the stadium, on the steps of the Propylaea, or amid the ruins of Mycenae, there were no statues. There were only columns, walls, gates, as in Luxor, Karnak, Dendara; and all the same, Greek temples aren't so different from Egyptian ones . . . How can I therefore understand my emotional preferences, since I initially trust them, more than any knowledge?

*

After all, wasn't it just as extraordinary to discover the colossuses of Abu Simbel sitting serenely, like sovereign incorruptible guards, across from the dazzling water of Lake Nasser and the black-sand pyramids that can be made out beyond it? Or to glimpse the noble and supple crown of palm trees between the enormous column shafts of Karnak that imitate their trunks? Hadn't I become, all the same, against my wishes, greedier with my feelings over the years, less permeable?

I'm nonetheless seeking other, more fertile, reasons. Olympia, for example: the first time that I felt so fulfilled in that site was surely due to the great oak trees, the olive trees, the nearby presence of the Alfeios River, all of which lent to the ruins their extraordinary appeasing power; I felt at home there, as it were, because of a nature similar to the one in which I'll have lived all my life and of a history that had pervaded me when I was very young without its thereafter losing any of its influence on me. The desert has a sublime quality; it fascinates me like a temptation (one is never fascinated by one's native land); but it will always remain for me, like the ocean, remote if not foreign.

*

The question of dimensions also surely matters. Statues, pylons and colossal temples obviously had to be raised in order to stand in victorious opposition to the desert. Their enormous dimensions are impressive; like the idea of having a genuine mountain built out of blocks in the hopes of guaranteeing the survival of corpses which, royal as they were, were no less frail than a bundle of bones. This surprised me as much as anyone, but like an enigma that remains at a distance.

*

Something else: although we were in an intensely sunny country that had long turned the sun into the supreme god, I don't know why the temples and the tombs possessed, to my eyes, something nocturnal about them; whereas as I walked up the steps of the Propylaea, beneath nearly the same sun, I had the impression of seeing the most diurnal light of the world concentrate and vibrate in the sort of crystal die that is the little temple of Athena Nike.

(Egyptian temples are sand-coloured, earth-coloured. Oddly, the temple that moved me the most, the Mortuary Temple of Ramesses III at Medinet Habu, has the same grey colour as, and in fact resembles, the mountain in the background. Oddly, indeed; and in regard to this preference one can measure the great proportion of arbitrariness and subjectivity in these remarks. Examining the guidebook, I learnt that the entrance, called the Royal Pavilion, to this temple at which, it must be added, there are relatively few visitors, was probably a triumphal gate 'of an entirely military character and imitated from the Asiatic fortresses of which Ramesses III had besieged'. Yet if I try to comprehend what spoke to me there more than elsewhere, I find two elements: first, in fact, this entrance with its storeys, specifically those small windows on the first storey through which one could make out a decorated ceiling, all of which gave to the entire pavilion—how to put it?—a kind of latent life, as if someone, a priest, a slave or a soldier, could still have appeared at one of those openings; and, second, something in fact military-like, which was in harmony with the third touching element, for me, of this temple, notably its location at the foot of a mountain and seemingly at the end of the world. So that my reverie—nourished again, a little farther on in the 'Great Temple', by the presence of immense engraved inscriptions which made me think, who knows why, of China—of a remote outpost at the border of an empire—mere reverie, of course, like the one that makes *The Desert of the Tartars* so priceless—resurged mutely, irresistibly in me, however groundless it was.)

The marble of Greek temples is captive light: their columns give no impression of being heavy and, between them, let the daylight circulate extensively. (It's true that we don't see them at all as they used to be, when they were also covered to protect and hide the god.) The love that one can feel for places and works of art depend on no lesser, and no less subterranean, nuances than as for any kind of love.

*

Having always been so uncertain about nearly every-thing, I find myself being quite assertive here, as if I'd finally chosen sides: the diurnal divinities instead of the nocturnal ones, the god with a human face instead of the army of masked gods unaware of passing time. The preceding pages demand revision; not out of prudence but, rather, so as not to fall into the narrow-mindedness of hasty irrevocable judgements.

Also seen during this same trip was a restored mortuary boat more than 40 metres long, made out of Lebanese cedar, and sheltered inside a sort of concrete keelson to the south of the Cheops Pyramid—a boat of which it is unknown whether it was used for the funerals of kings, for ritual pilgrimages on the Nile, or if it was also, like so many other religious represen-tations, supposed to bear the royal remains into the Beyond.

In front of this admirable object, like the other ones making up the treasures of Tutankhamun* or the

---

* First and foremost among the reasons explaining the fascination exerted by the treasures of Tutankhamun on so many visitors of the Cairo Museum is, of course, their funereal character, not to mention the picturesque circumstances of their discovery. That all the objects were found, intact, in a tomb (and not just any tomb), that they had been buried there less to preserve them greedily or devoutly than ever with the insane hope that that they could be put to use by the dead pharaoh show a madness that dis-turbs us and lends to all this paraphernalia what must be called an aura. Moreover, many of the treasures are black and gold, and therefore simply and sovereignly sum up an opposition between

wood panels of Hesy-Ra,* the mind finds itself
gripped by stupor; despite everything, little would be

the sun and shadows, between what is richest, brightest and what
is most threatening, nocturnal, impassable, a combat that hasn't
completely ceased being ours. And there's more. I intensely
observed those thrones, those jewellery cases, those parade beds,
those chariots. Why do they seem admirable to such an extent,
whereas the canopy beds, thrones and coaches of our kings,
although they can dazzle us with their luxury, leave us unaf-
fected? Those utterly simple chariots, those condensed chariots
seemingly conceived from the onset for ghosts of horses,
shades of princes, absences; those chariots similar to hieroglyphs
meaning 'chariot', reduced by a prodigious sense of abbreviation
to the purest and most elegant sign that would indicate racing,
hunting, conquest . . . One would almost come to believe, however unreasonable this may seem, that if ever vehicles, built with
human hands, had been able to cross the last threshold, they'd
have been those chariots; and those boats as well . . .

* That dead man, probably a scribe according to his attributes—
a writing case and a reed pen—had his tomb near the pyramid
of Djoser, at Saqqara. Nearly forty-seven centuries ago, as for
all the great figures of his time, one wanted to ensure his entry
into the world of stars and gods by representing him on wood
panels, three of which, if I'm not mistaken, are visible in the
Museum of Cairo. The dark yet warm colour of the wood (as if
it were still reflecting a fire), the natural veins and the chipped
paint, the cracks that time had inflicted on him, lend to a particularly pure and noble stylization just what is needed by way of
alteration, that is, of life, in order to make it more mysterious and
moving than elsewhere. It's on the threshold of these door-like
passages, on which every engraved letter is like the key of an
extraordinary night music, that I could fall, despite everything,
under the power of those images; but I no longer really wish this
to happen.

needed to enable the nostalgia for the magical thinking that permitted the invention and fabrication of these objects and these enormous extravagant monuments—since they show, on a big scale, the dream or the illusion of going through the gates of death—to grasp us, because a deep beauty is inseparable from it. (I'd also experienced this, long ago, in the Etruscan tombs of Cerveteri, so similar to those of Thebes.)

Indeed, when I think about it, I must correct myself; what sometimes links us to this world anterior to smiling, to history, to time, and to drama, all those inscriptions, all those figures that look so much like constellations engraved on the night and seemingly on the surface of an incomprehensible abyss, still speak to me with force; perhaps even, for some of them, as much as they used to. But what has probably taken place is that I better measure both the enormous distance separating me from that world and the proximity of the world, completely permeated by two lights—Greek and Christian—in which I was raised and live. More clearly than ever, I see that I wouldn't know how to don the getup of the priests of Horus (even if they'd also gone through a kind of *aggiornamento*). I wouldn't even be able, and I regret this, to convert myself to the kind of eternity which is made more admirably audible than any other by the Georgian liturgy, which cannot be saved from the destruction promised to every work of art in this world, even if it had been the most faithful reflection of another world that eludes us. Such are forms which are, strictly speaking, sublime, yet which can only distance themselves more or less slowly, painfully, from us, while we know that they've been the closest to what we'd still like to call The Highest, which won't cease being our aim.

*

Absolutely no temple remains, at the end of this millennium, where one can turn oneself into an officiating priest or a supplicant without making a conscious effort, without running the risk, as it were, of betraying oneself. Even if they all were, in all places and in all times, the most beautiful dwelling places imaginable (we have this feeling even in the most ruined ones). As if Osiris had once again been torn apart and were no longer healable. One can no longer sing in a choir. All the same, strangely enough, the silence is still not complete, nor the despair absolute. One still tries to speak a language in which the inevitable nostalgia for hymns, for all kinds of hymns, including the most ancient ones, instead of wilting into sterile plaintive songs or imitations, would nourish, like a dark soil, a few seeds just viable enough to venture into the likewise dark, unspecified space of the future; and these seeds wouldn't be able to do so unless we speak more rigorously and genuinely than ever before, in accordance with what we are, lost, not understanding anything of anything or only a very little, yet fully alive all the same, strangely alive in spite of everything; still breathing; even capable of laughing occasionally; perhaps because what made the temples rise—temples that we've subsequently watched collapsing one after the other—seemingly persists, against all likelihood, in a different way. Would it then be that the nostalgia we can feel for the sacred isn't simply a way of turning around, of looking behind us? It's as if this something that had irrefutably made Karnak, the Acropolis, or Chartres rise, that had made them blossom, were still, paradoxically, ahead of us. This is difficult to think about and thus to defend, and to express. It's surely impossible to explain, even more impossible to prove (if there are degrees of impossibility, and if proofs are needed). As if the divine light (let's thus call it that, for lack of anything better) were not only behind us, forever, projecting in front of our eyes our own shadow like an obsessive image of our death, but also could not *not* still be ahead of us, different, scattered, by no means promised, yet by no means annihilated either; barely detectable, graspable, conceivable . . .

So I imagine this face, whatever it is, as ours, warmed all the same, blushed pink all the same by these debris of the morning sun, confident because it won't see its shadow any more, once again and perhaps forever, as only behind it.

(1992)

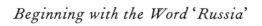

Beginning with the Word 'Russia'

To Pierre and Olga Morel

To the word 'Russia' were initially linked in my mind only a few images, drawn from my reading, while a child, of Jules Verne's *Michel Strogoff* in the large Hetzel edition with its red-and-gold cover. I'd of course loved that book, indeed passionately, because of its dramatic and delightfully moving story, that of a long battle between good and evil, led (to an overtly predictable victory) by a hero as noble in heart, as perfect as (in another unforgettable book) Athos, my favourite among the Musketeers (even if I also loved Artagnan's brio and Aramis' slyer seductiveness). But the story of Michel Strogoff could have taken place elsewhere in the world in a no less lively and convincing manner; and when all is said and done, its heroes had little that was specifically Russian about them. Indeed, what, in that book, has remained linked in my mind, for my entire life, to Russia are merely a few words and a few images; place names whose harsh, even brutal sonority—Omsk, Tomsk, Irkoutsk—was enough to make them strange and to make he who heard them journey afar, even before he knew anything about them; names of things as well, more specific words—*telega*, *tarantass*, *knout*; the latter word especially, where the *k* that ends so many Russian proper nouns clacked at the beginning like the very crack of a whip streaking a victim's back or face, the *knout* thus doubtless getting engraved in me as one of the emblems of imperial Russia; with the word 'czar' that Jules Verne uses in French, so much more graphic than the better-made 'tsar' of contemporary French, the lightning bolt of the z evoking a remote and all-mighty sovereign capable of the best and the worst; this czar who appears for the first time in the book as an almost self-effacing officer of the guard, under the brightly shining chandeliers of the great ballroom of the New Palace; but turning his back on those bright lights, in the first, never forgotten illustration of the book, with this caption: 'He came to take a breath of air on the wide balcony'; a martial and severe-looking personage, puffing out his chest below his tunic festooned with brandeburgs while the child-reader discovers further to the left, beneath the starry sky, a few church domes and, especially, at the sovereign's feet, two galloping horsemen, dark shapes nervous like crows and, like them, seemingly forewarning of some certain evil . . .

(I still wonder what those so modestly, so legitimately illustrative illustrations draw their power from—Max Ernst made marvellous use of them. No photograph could equal them; but neither would engravings by great artists; or the result would be something completely different. This is why, for example, the illustration of the Nizhny-Novgorod Fair, with this caption—'There was movement, excitement'—has remained present to my mind all my life, to the extent that I cannot hear *Petrushka* without seeing it again. The captions themselves contribute to the magical effect, perhaps because they're most often composed of truncated, suspended sentences, at once linked to the story and leaving an open space, a potential, a future in front of them. All the same, it's not excluded that old photographs exert an analogous charm, situated, as they are, between exactness and inexactness, a copy and a transposition; nor are they 'perfect'; and they're often anonymous; the chiaroscuro, in both cases, adds to the mystery.)

Only a few signs thus sufficed to create an at-once disturbing and fabulous distant land: the presence of a bear, threatening in the mountains or comical in a circus parade; a troupe of messy Gypsies with grim, rather aggressive looks on their faces; log cabins, onion-shaped belfries. With all that, a background of vast wilderness expanses to cross, violent confrontations with the elements, wild animals, an avowed or concealed enemy.

For the first time, a vast expanse to the east of the heart opened up for me as I was reading, thanks to the power of the names and the imagery, thanks as well to maps specifying the itinerary of the indomitable messenger, as if one couldn't really doubt for an instant that it was a true story. Today, I tell myself that this expanse, this reserve of the unknown, might just as well have opened up, after all, to the west (in the remote West of James Fenimore Cooper's redskins), to the north (in the Yukon and Northwest Territories of *White Fang*), or to the south in the desert or the African savannah. Yet cowboy and Indian stories almost always left me indifferent; the desert still didn't have anything to say to me; any jungle suffocated me at the mere sound of the word; and tales from the polar regions already bored me so much that I still find almost incomprehensible any attraction to those icy landscapes. It must thus be true that something in me was and still is made for turning me towards the Levant, even if I resign myself, without much pain, to not yielding to this attraction to the extent of wanting to go there and verify it on the spot; this 'there' being, in fact, vast and vague, since it begins in Central Europe, follows in Michel Strogoff's footsteps and could extend, by means of the Trans-Siberian Railway or the caravan route, all the way to China; but it could extend just as well to old Persia, to Nepal, to Tibet, and, less irresistibly, to India.

There's no great mystery behind this predilection: for my reverie to get attached to a place, there needs to be, besides vast expanses and wilderness reserves, the memory, if not the survival, of a high culture. As for those geographical maps where colours enable one to distinguish, at first glance, deserts, forests, mountains and seas, as well as geological and climatic zones, I could draw a map on which the density, the complexity and the level of the cultures of the human mind would also be inscribed. Today, I'm not unaware of how unjust it would be to neglect the cultures of Black Africa or the Aztecs, as it would be to forget that the American Indians and the Eskimos also have an art. But to be specific, the question for me is not to know everything or to be equitable; here I'm only recovering the readings, reveries and passions from my childhood or adolescence; and I've just been wondering, as the booklover I've always been, whether I could have even imagined a culture that it had been impossible to collect and preserve, as time went by, in those beautiful beehives that are libraries with their thousands of teeming signs, like so many sometimes-productive bees. All those kinds of writing, all those great beautiful pages, decipherable or not, like so many sky charts, like signs between which an infinity would come into view. It thus indeed seems to me that back then, so many remote years ago, consciously or not, legitimately or not, were allied in my mind, to feed this vague élan towards the East, the same two inclinations which, later, attached me to the area where I live: a taste for wild landscapes and for culture, including the most refined forms, and already, without my knowing so, an attempt to bring them into harmony. With, in addition, the old magic of distance that has today lost its power as all distances are shortening.

(One must also not forget that, for us, it's on this side that the sun rises; and that the words 'orient' and 'origin' have the same root.)

Let me come back to Russia. For years, those few names of places and things, those few images, which are as insidious as scenes seen in dreams, must have remained my only links to the reality that is designated or, rather, had been designated under that name during Jules Verne's time and up to 1917. (And in the momentum that would again, in various periods of time, carry me towards that country, I could never call it by another name.)

I must have read, and just as soon tried to translate, some of Rilke's *Book of Hours* at the age of seventeen. There's no doubt that the first two sections of the volume, which result from Rilke's two Russian trips and consist of poems that, today, strike me as flowing from a movement that is rather too simplistic and abundant, also contributed to leading me back to the Russia I dreamt of. When the poems don't make their way, like the slow, monotonous and fervent (a little too fervent) pilgrims that they evoke, towards God, they go around in circles, like whispered prayers, around Him, a God whom Rilke imagined to be a tall, eternally growing tree, or an inexhaustible fountain, or a mountain, and who—so he was persuaded—was truly the Russian God. As for myself, who was reading at the time those poems with a vague fervour similar to the one that had produced them, they once again opened onto, by means of the name 'Russia', a boundless, rather grey, deep expanse from which only words as vast and solemn as the country could reach me. I'd imagine that immense cathedral, those tolling bells and bellowing flooding rivers, those pious, stooping, infinitely patient crowds; one would be tempted to believe that those images were more dreamt of than real; however, not too long ago, a documentary film devoted to the survival of the Orthodox Church in the USSR showed pilgrims, worn-out but happy, reaching their goal—a yellow convent in the snow—and they could have faithfully illustrated such images.

Now I don't intend to go over once again, with a slower step and a more attentive, more mature, more critical gaze, all those acres of Russian literature in which I so much loved going astray. I'm trying to recover only a few images, the most persistent ones. For example, that short story by Chekhov, 'Easter Eve', discovered in 1948 in the paperback collection that the Éditions Mermod had then initiated and quickly abandoned (the translator's name isn't mentioned, but it seems to me that I heard back then that this version had been made by Charles Ferdinand Ramuz with the help of Mermod's Russian wife).

The narrator is waiting for a ferryboat that should enable him to attend Easter celebrations in a monastery located on the opposite bank; the ferryman is a young monk from this monastery. During the crossing, he confides his sorrow in the narrator: the archdeacon Nicolay, whose mild character is equalled only by his talent at composing canticles in praise of the Virgin and the saints, has just died; he'd shown an almost maternal affection for the young brother. Everything that is said in these pages, and said—this is essential—almost in hushed tones, with perfect simplicity—the river crossing, the springtime flooding, the fires burning for the celebrations in the haze and the dark night, the droning bells, the perceptible presence of a jubilant crowd, the melancholy separation, the fragments of canticles that the young monk quotes to the glory of the pure Word—all this brings as many themes and motifs (to which everyone is especially sensitive) together into a sort of fluid, deeply inner polyphony that seemingly bears the affirmation of the Resurrection.

(This story joins my memory of another evocation of Easter Eve, a memory so vague that I no longer know where to find its source, but this matters little: my mind retains the images of ice breaking up in a river and of kisses exchanged by the faithful at the end of a church service, at dawn, while they're also passing around, like another dawn, another holy host, the most joyous words: 'Christ has risen.'*)

---

* In fact, I must have brought together two passages of [Tolstoy's] *Resurrection* that follow closely upon each other but are not simultaneous: Easter Eve, in Chapter 15, when Nekhlyudov meets the young Katyusha in the church and then

This polyphony, therefore, but the word is unsuitable, this knotting, this fusion of themes, and the word 'theme' leads one astray as well because everything is simpler, more interior, more down-to-earth, this fusion of experienced images corresponded to deep dreams of which I wasn't even aware: crossing a river—while this river is casting off chains of ice, making the hems of its breastplate crack and its voice swell like organ music to celebrate the force of spring—towards another bank where an at-once musical and luminous celebration would be taking place; watching fires getting lit in the haze and the darkness; hearing words, or even just hearing people talking, in this same night, with absolutely pure words into which tenderness, consolation and gentle triumph were woven; floating slowly towards the daylight while coming out of the fog like a dead man from his wrappings ('We floated across, disturbing on our way the lazily lifting fog'—without forgetting, but how would it be possible to forget?—the 'rosy face with black eyebrows' of the young merchant woman from whom the ferryman, thinking of his dead friend, cannot remove his eyes): moreover—let me insist on this—it was almost without vibrato and bombast that these few pages were announcing, raising the highest and most secret hope that can be nurtured. (And in the recomposed memory told in *Resurrection*, more or

the night of Chapter 17 when he meets her in her bedroom while the ice is breaking up and rumbling outside in the fog.

less the same images were combined under the same sign: the candle flames and the kisses for peace against a background of darkness lifting and tumultuous, unshackled waters as powerful as rising from the grave . . . I wonder if the man who I am, had I been born and raised in that world, might have believed the Word and repeated it with the same joy, in spite of all reason, because it was no less absurd back then than today when I listen to it in a truly foreign and unpronounceable language. To the extent of believing that there would be privileged places and moments, even for truths proclaimed 'eternal'.)

I still have the impression of hearing right now, after a half-century (almost the life of a human being), the voice of Hugues Cuénod, playing the role of the evangelist in the St Matthew Passion, at the tribune of a church in Lausanne, singing the tale of St Peter's denial of Christ: 'Und ging heraus, und weinete bitterlich' (and this isn't only because this was the first time that no other voice, later, could erase Cuénod's from my memory). But, thanks (or not) to Bach, it's the whole scene that I still have the impression of seeing with my very own eyes, like the scenes which one discovers in the background of some of Tintoretto's great paintings and on which one more willingly gazes than on the foreground. It's night in the courtyard of the Palace of Caiaphas, and, because the weather is still chilly—it's the beginning of spring—in a corner there's a burning fire around which are gathered a few guardians whom Peter has joined, waiting to see 'what will happen'. One also discovers, as in this Tintoretto painting that I'm imagining, one or two servant women whom the fire, or the presence of the guardians, or, more likely, the excitation brought about by what is happening, has lured outside; and because they're young women, their presence also glows in this night at the end of winter. It seems to me that I see them and that I could brush up against one of them on the threshold. The night is coming to an end: it's the moment when a shivering of tiredness attains even the hardiest person, the most difficult moment in the darkness. Even in broad daylight, in fact, it's not easy not to be cowardly or simply not to hesitate, not to doubt. Upon this, suddenly rises the cock's crow, which, in German, in Luther's German, truly creaks like an iron door that opens onto, or closes off, something that remains unknown. Then bitter weeping bursts out just at dawn, at sunrise. All this is tied up very tightly into a knot, like the flavours of a dish to nourish all of one's being; like a knot in the cloth of time, of history, a condensation of everything essential that can be experienced by a human being; at the same time, it's never anything but a real scene where the cold air at the end of the night rubs against the rough walls of a courtyard, the rough cloth of the clothes, and against the hands, the feet, the faces. And the unforgettable musical phrase, heard every time with the same emotion once again, is as if you were falling flat on your face; yet at the same time as you fall, the melody picks you back up, sets you back on your feet, just as a servant woman would do, instead of denouncing you.

What is all this, however? A few words, a few musical notes, nothing but an inflexion which, so I notice, being free from any devotion, have been gathered inside oneself if not forever, then at least for as long as one will keep breathing or, at least, be conscious.

'And he went out, and wept bitterly.'

To my mind, there's a link between this man who turns his back to us but without being able to hide his tears, this exalted man who believed himself to be stronger than the others and who is actually too weak, and Dostoyevsky's characters whom I encountered for the first time during those same war years and, without being aware of it, by no means viewed as characters of books, as engaged in vain fictional tales. They existed, somewhere; I didn't know where, nor cared about knowing; they existed much more than many human beings with whom I rubbed shoulders day after day.

Christ was present in Bach's *Passion* more than in any sermon, any kind of worship, any of those cold Protestant churches which I still sometimes entered, because Bach's genius was deep enough to meet Him; and He was also in Dostoyevsky's pages in another way, because their worlds were very remote from each other yet in a no less convincing way.

Now that I think about it: Dostoyevsky's reader doesn't see much of Russia; not only nearly nothing of the landscapes, of nature, but also not much of the cities, even the interiors where the plot takes place (if one recalls the minutely detailed descriptions of a Balzac, for example). His soul isn't tranquil enough, not serene enough, to linger over such matters. His inner fervour leaves him no time for them. When I recall his books, I see little more than night, snow, mud, dark streets and stairways, many stairways, sometimes bright salons, more often smoky rooms of inns, dives and hovels; and inside them, what haunts the novelist's gaze are human beings whose inner darkness reflects, increases, the darkness in which they can themselves be barely made out, just their faces being at once intensely present and ungraspable, almost always caught in their movements, if not when losing their balance because the ground is slipping out from under their feet. One might think of Rembrandt, in whose work faces are also contaminated by darkness (and if they shine, it's because of a light that seems to emanate from inside them); yet nothing in his painting recalls instability, feverish violence, the sometimes frenzied exaltation of the human beings whom the novelist carried inside him.

Those characters are especially faces: especially looks; and much speaking, floods of words that are often frantic and that nothing can stop; blended with many tears, rarer laughter, much crying out. In real life, one wouldn't be able to bear those fanatics very long. Why did I listen to them, back then, more passionately than all the others, why did I love them to that extent? This could be because they cried out a little like children or adolescents, an absolutely pure crying out (even ending up in impurity); like Rimbaud, to whom I paid, during those same years, the same impassioned attention.

The *De Profundis* is the Latin version, used in the funeral liturgy, of Psalm 130: 'Out of the depths have I cried unto thee, O Lord.' The Latin has become too beautiful for our day and age. Boris de Schloezer, translating Dostoïevski (as his name is now transliterated into French) in 1926, before the writer's name had lost its *y*, used *La Voix souterraine* ('The Underground Voice') as a title for what today has become *Notes d'un souterrain* ('Notes from an Underground' or 'Notes from an Underground Man'). This is because the word 'voix' ('voice') was still too beautiful. But shouldn't one go all the way and replace 'souterrain' ('underground') by 'sous-sol' ('basement'), a word that is more terse and prosaic?

I bought *La Voix souterraine* in 1945. The book is tattered, the margins marked with single, double, even triple lines, something that has never been, even back then, among my reading habits. This is because this book is truly our *De Profundis*; but the crying out is worse since it's no longer addressed to anyone and since he who is crying out no longer knows whether he is someone; since he's tearing himself apart, turning against himself, and now has no other certitude than the wall that he comes up against. (Job 19:8, already: 'He hath fenced up my way that I cannot pass.')

Perhaps Leopardi alone, before Dostoyevsky, saw such darkness in our fate: 'Everything is evil. That is to say, everything that is, is evil; that everything exists is an evil; everything exists for an evil end; existence is an evil and directed towards evil; the goal of the universe is evil; the order and the State, the laws and the natural course of the universe are nothing but evil and aim at evil. There is no other good than nonbeing; there is nothing good except that which is not; things that are not things; all things are bad.' (*Zibaldone*, Bologna, 22 April 1826.)

The *Notes from Underground* are the recriminations, the cries of a man who has come up against the wall of the 'natural laws', the purely rational, mathematical laws that rule over nature, the wall of

'2 x 2 = 4', and he's horrified that this wall is at once indestructible and inacceptable; that there's an absolute, definitive incompatibility between the living individual (who I am) and the uninhabitable order of reason and science, the order of the modern world as Dostoyevsky saw it little by little taking shape and acquiring power, similar to a monstrous machine in which he on no account wished to become a cog. (What would he say today, a hundred years later? Would he still have the courage to speak out? Would he speak like Beckett?)

Three years after *Notes from Underground*, in *The Idiot*, young Hippolyte, suffering from consumption and knowing his death to be near, takes up again in a more explicit and, to a certain extent, calmer manner the same protestation, with the bitter vehemence of one who has banged his forehead against the wall. (In a more explicit and perhaps rather less immediately convincing manner than in *Notes from Underground*, because this voice no longer speaks alone and must come to terms with others who are supposed to respond to it, refute it, or refine it.) This raging complaint ('I cannot submit myself to a dark force that takes on the shape of a tarantula' . . . 'What is this moral doctrine that demands, besides your life, even that last gasp with which you give over the last atom of your life' . . . 'What do I need all this beauty for when I must now know, I'm obliged to know in every minute, in every instant, that this minute gnat itself that is buzzing around me in a ray of sunlight takes part in this feast, knows its place, likes it and is happy about it, and that I'm alone, the only one to be rejected from it . . . ' passage in which one cannot help but remember Rimbaud: 'Oh! the drunken gnat in the inn urinal, in love with borage, and dissolved by a ray of sunlight!'), this complaint, this protestation, has been taken up again ever since then, consciously or not, in numerous other books. I don't believe that it has ever risen so purely, so truthfully, so heartrendingly; because it was, in a certain sense, the first protestation; and because Dostoyevsky knew at first hand the basement, the mud, the darkness, since he bore them along inside himself.

In Hippolyte's confession, the revolt could have targeted only an anonymous God, responsible for the wall. But there's something else. At the merchant Rogozhin's, Hippolyte has seen a painting, a copy of Holbein's *Dead Christ*, in other words, that unthinkable thing that is the corpse of a God. Myshkin had already confided in his friend, the owner of the canvas, that the painting was enough to make people lose their faith. Hippolyte confirms this: 'Then unwillingly emerged the idea that if death is so horrible and the laws of nature so powerful, then how can one get to the end of them? How can they be overcome when He was unable to vanquish them, He who during his lifetime had triumphed over Nature, which obeyed Him? [. . .] The people who were surrounding the corpse, none of whom are shown on the canvas, must have felt atrocious anguish and confusion during an evening that shattered in one blow their hopes and almost even their beliefs. [. . .] And if the Master Himself had been able to see His own image, on the eve of his agonies, would He have gone up on the cross and would He have died as He was?'

No one in the book responds to Hippolyte that all hope could lie therein, on the contrary: in this corpse of a God who was spared nothing of human suffering.

Dostoyevsky died on 27 January 1881. The next year appeared *The Gay Science*, with this other cry, destined to ring out long and powerfully, the cry of the 'insane' man: 'Where is God? I'm going to tell you! *We have killed him*—you and me! We're his murderers! But how did we do that? How were we able to drain the sea? Who gave us the sponge for erasing the whole horizon? What have we done to disenchant this earth of its sun? Where is it now spinning off to? Where are we carrying its movement to? Far from all the suns? Haven't we rushed into a continuous fall? And backwards, sideways, forwards, to all sides? Is there still an up and a down? Aren't we wandering as if across an infinite nothingness? Don't we feel the breath of emptiness? Isn't it colder? Isn't it ever night and more and more night? Don't we already have to light the streetlamps in the morning? Have we still not heard anything of the noise of the gravediggers who have buried God? Have we still not smelt anything of the divine putrefaction? Gods also rot! God is dead! God stays dead! And we're the ones who killed Him!'. . .

When you're an adolescent and some leftover Protestantism obliges you to accept the ritual, nearly void of any kind of meaning, of 'religious education', how could you have loved the suave Christ of pious imagery, the 'little Jesus', the 'good shepherd', whereas you'd so willingly have taken up Rimbaud's exclamation against 'the eternal thief of energies'? I won't linger today over this rather superficial liking for Hell, for hells, that nourished a hardly less superficial reading of 'accursed poets'. As to the bloody Christs of Spain and Grünewald's *Crucifixion of Christ*, they frightened me; instinctively, I couldn't accept that the image of a tortured man could illuminate our lives. (Today, I could begin to understand this better; I don't accept it, but I've begun to understand the depths in which that tree has taken root.) Even if one had wished, back then, to cross that thick surface of clichés, to correct that long wearing down, that long dulling of initially fresh and subversive words, one wouldn't have been able to do so, not knowing how to proceed (and surely not by getting any help from electric guitars). Rather more helpful, if one had been become aware of them, were so-called works of art like Bach's *Passion* or those great novels dominated by Christ-like figures, *Don Quixote* or *The Idiot*.

In his *Dostoïevki par lui-même*, Dominique Arban shows how, if not the discovery, then at least a new encounter with the main character of *Don Quixote*, during a lecture given by Turgenev in 1860 (only twenty-odd days after Dostoyevsky had returned from Siberia), lecture in which Cervantes' hero was presented as a human reincarnation of Christ, might have contributed to the invention of *The Idiot*, in which, according to the author himself, 'the essential idea is to create an absolutely good man, Christ'. Twenty years later, in his *Writer's Diary*, Dostoyevsky will write apropos of Don Quixote: 'the most magnanimous of all the knights who lived in the world, the most ingenuous soul and, as to his heart, one of the greatest that the earth has ever borne'; and of the book itself: 'this book, the saddest of all [. . .], a witness to what was the deepest mystery, the fatal mystery, of man and mankind.'

And indeed, despite all the deep differences between the two works, the same Christ-like light (the true light, without mellowness and equivocation) illumines the two fictional characters, who are nearly immortal for us, Don Quixote and Prince Myshkin, whom we'd prefer re-naming 'the innocent one' instead of 'the idiot'.

The kinship between them is, moreover, vouched for in the novel itself by the scene where there's an allusion to the 'poor knight', the hero of one of

Pushkin's poems in which it's understood, early on, that he designates the prince whom the Yepanchin sisters mock so affectionately. And when their mother, the general's wife, irritated by these allusions that she doesn't understand, asks Aglaya who this 'poor knight' is, she replies: 'The poor knight is Don Quixote, a Don Quixote who isn't comical, but serious'; and. to specify his character traits: 'a man capable of having an ideal and, having established one for himself, of devoting himself to it for his lifetime'.

If Mushkin is a genuine prince, he's in fact a poor man. When he first appears in the novel, in the compartment of the Warsaw–Saint Petersburg train, what initially strikes his travelling companions (and us, who will be following him much longer) is his poverty, besides his scrawny physique and his sickly air: 'He was holding a little bundle enveloped in a faded scarf, and this was apparently all his luggage.' And this is indeed what, a little later, when he arrives at the house of the general's wife, whom he knows is one of his distant relatives, will induce the butler ordered to welcome the visitors to look at him so suspiciously: ' "Wait in this antechamber and leave your little package here," he says deliberately while sitting down in an armchair and casting a severe look at the prince who had sat down unaffectedly on the nearby chair, his bundle of clothes in his hand.'

From this very first scene in the novel, the reader, through the conversation of the three men who are sharing the same train compartment in the cold and tiredness of the end of their trip and about whom he still knows nothing, will have grasped a few fragments of the story that deeply explores, even though the novel has barely begun, a sort of feverish maelstrom around a centre that one can still only glimpse, where thousands of roubles and jewels are shining, even as knives will also soon shine, more than once; where a woman's name is pronounced for the first time, Anastassya Filippovna, not yet seen like Helen, when the old men praise her on the ramparts of Troy, and like her already passionately admired and followed. (Except that the Trojan War, in *The Iliad*, is a ceremony that takes place in a world whose sovereign order remains undisturbed by even the violent death of soldiers, whereas the slightest incident here— even the more light-hearted scenes where laughter occurs—takes place in a world that has lost its foundations and where no festivity concludes without trouble, if it doesn't verge on disaster.)

'More light-hearted scenes': here's one, indeed, that follows upon the preceding one, the unexpected arrival of the prince at the Yepanchins', where he falls into a complete untidiness as well, but a comical untidiness; to end up, as we've seen, not without difficulty, so shabby is his appearance in the salon where the general and his three daughters are letting themselves be swept away with ravishment in the merriest swirling dances. There, in front of a charming tribunal consisting of this lady and her daughters, without taking offence at their laughter which isn't, however, lacking in impertinence with respect to him, and in fact laughing with them at his oafishness, the prince unsurprisingly soon opens his heart to them; and to their warm welcome, he responds by immediately confiding his most anguishing as well as his most luminous experiences. 'He's a genuine child, even a pitiful one,' the general had said when introducing the prince to his wife. Surely an innocent man ('You'll be ashamed, Ganka, to have insulted such a . . . sheep—he couldn't find another word,' Rogozhin will say much later) more than an idiot; a child who never feels more at ease than when in the company of children. In the Yepanchins' salon, he seemingly soon forgets where he is, to whom he is speaking, and this is also why his charm is irresistible. The at-once affectionate and mocking laughter of the girls listening to him with astonishment is seemingly echoed, in his memories of Switzerland—and it's not unimportant that he has returned from that country, still considered to be the cradle of liberty and a new Arcadia—by the noise of the waterfall that he loved listening to at night, his privileged relationship with the children ('I'd tell them everything, I'd hide nothing from them': one has the impression of hearing Rousseau, and Hölderlin after him), and the luminous story of one Maria saved from calamity indeed by children.

Alyosha will also have, in *The Brothers Karamazov*, privileged relationships with children. And when at the very end of that book full of darkness, during young Ilyusha's burial, he speaks to his companions and calls them 'my doves' ('let me use this name for you, since you look like charming birds'), one forgets that this metaphor is ordinary in Russian; one is even led beyond the resemblance that Alyosha himself underscores, one really sees the sign of a white bird opening on the page and retrospectively illuminating the whole book, however dark it has been, like the dove of Noah's Ark or the one spreading its bright-white wings above the Christ in Piero della Francesca's *Baptism of Christ*.

In the first part of *The Brothers Karamazov*, where, even more so than in *The Idiot*, the reader is swept away by the storm of the most violent passions, at the end, after Dmitri Karamazov, emerging from the shadows in front of his brother Alyosha, has summed up the horror of his state by means of this singular phrase: 'the mire is a fury' (at least in Henri Mongault's translation), the younger brother goes back to the monastery where venerable Father Zossima is dying; the storm calms down; but the true clear weather of this ending is less the religious serenity that produces it than a short love letter written by Lisa Hohlakov to Alyosha: 'Alexis Fyodorovitch, what will happen if I can't keep myself from laughing when I see you, like this morning? You'll take me for a merciless mocker and will have doubts about my letter. This is why I beg you, my dearest, not to look at me too much when you come since I might burst out laughing at the sight of your long robe'. And Dostoyevsky adds: 'Alyosha read this letter twice, with surprise, remained pensive, then softly chuckled with pleasure. He shivered, feeling guilty about his chuckling. But, after a moment, he once again chuckled, happily'.

The surprise of this blend of tenderness and merriment is, strictly speaking, clear water after the 'fury of the mire'.

Exactly the same case obtains in *The Idiot* with the character of Aglaya Yepanchin (whose first name meant 'brightness, beauty, finery' in Greek), who is also tender and cheerful. However, there's a crucial moment in the novel when her laughter rings out again: after Hippolyte's confession and failed suicide. Prince Myshkin comes out of the house where the horrible senselessness of human life has just been vehemently denounced by the young sick man; he reaches the public garden, deeply moved by what he has heard; suddenly the memory of the mountains, the clear sky, with the idea of a possible happiness despite everything, arises in him; he recalls, as if it were he who had whispered them to Hippolyte, the latter's words apropos of the gnat who is happy because it knows what its place is in the natural scheme of things.

Then he dozes off; and despite the 'clear and majestic silence' surrounding him in the park, his dreams take on the colour of anguish; a woman, who isn't given a name but whose face, expressing repentance and dread, cannot be that of Anastassya Filippovna, appears and seems to want to lead him off. Then: 'He stood up to follow her, but a clear, fresh laugh suddenly sounded near him; a hand found itself in his; he grasped it, squeezed it and awoke. Aglaya was in front of him and laughing loudly.'

Elsewhere, during the tale, the prince will say to the same girl: 'What are you doing in the darkness?' When the mire changes into fury, that is, when baseness and violence truly fly into a rage like a storm, is there still a chance for clear water to cut a path? I'm not forgetting that Lev Shestov finds Prince Myshkin cowardly, because he resigns himself to the Law, and Alyosha vapid, in contrast to the crying out that he incessantly hears rising, in Dostoyevsky, from beneath the ground. For me, today, now that I have reread these great books, their clear, luminous moments did not seem less 'true' than the darkest ones; perhaps because I now happen, and only now, like Prince Myshkin, like the idiot, to recall the mountains of Switzerland where 'every morning, the rainbow takes shape above the waterfall', and because the clear laughter and beauty of Aglaya are not more unknown to me than to any other man in the world.

Nothing in the natural world more than a torrent resembles this ingenuous, though not angelic, not disincarnated, laughter: something has leapt out to meet you, less for assailing you than for quenching your thirst or washing you; someone runs towards you to ravish you; a breach has opened in the stone wall against which the skull would have ended up shattering; that surging water exempts you from any other key.

The depths of hell don't consist of fire. However fast and violent are its ravages, fire looks too much like a tiger; it too obviously has a tiger's claws and fur (I once saw it leaping like that behind my back) to represent the worst: it's too bright, has too much blood for that. It resembles a barbaric horde against which the battle seems not impossible, if not victory.

I remember reading *White Fang*, among so many other books, when I was a child; and I also remember that I didn't like that world without vegetation, without rivers, with almost no dwelling places, those almost empty expanses, that pale sun, and all that cold, all that ice, all that whiteness. I don't think that I ever read any other tales coming from polar climes. Whenever they were evoked, perhaps was still floating in my memory an engraving from Camille Flammarion's *L'Astronomie populaire*, in which, among several representations of possible ends of the world, skeletons in an icy cave depicted an end of the world through coldness.

However, in recent years, because of other books read sometimes by chance and without intending to do so whatsoever, I've mentally had to follow a path of coldness, a path towards ever-more coldness that a probably-too-lenient fate has spared my own feet.

The first landmark along this path, raised in 1975 in the review *Argile* thanks to the translator Jean-Claude Schneider, was Osip Mandelstam's famous poem from 1921: 'I was washing myself at night in the yard', apropos of which I later quoted Simone Weil: 'Wounds: it's the business of living that enters the body. May any suffering bring the universe into the body.'

In 1981, when I took on the risk of translating him in turn, and of writing about him, I observed that he'd struck me like a meteor, at once hard and brilliant, something that had come from afar, implacable, yet sensed at the same time as a kind of *proof* (that poetry, even today, kept all its meaning) and as a *model*, however inimitable.

In question is a cold night, of hard and sharp-edged things; in question is what chills, but not only the body. Night and frost also come from man, are seemingly blown against us through man's power. We haven't experienced that, at least in the same way and with the same violence here, in our temperate climes (where there has been and still is room for other hardships); this poem had to come to us from Soviet

Russia, written only four years after the beginning of the Revolution which even a man as little 'politicized' as my compatriot Charles Ferdinand Ramuz had considered to be 'The Great Spring', along with so many others who believed this longer than he did. Yet what this poem says still concerns only the first circle of cold; the circle where the cold can be mastered, when it's faced up to, and turned into something good. In this first circle, the cold strips bare, but makes things shine; it purifies things by reducing them to their core; the earth where we live, turned more aggressive because of the cold, becomes all the truer. From a similar collision, a kind of joy can be extracted as incontestable as the spark leaping froth from a piece of flint.

In such hands, language becomes leaner and stronger.

Mandelstam gripped this block of words in his fist; because he could do so, he was also able to maintain, almost to the end, the warmth of his lyricism when he descended into harsher circles. He didn't like the cold; he liked the leonine sun of Armenia and the bright colours of the French impressionists.

To make him stop speaking, he had to be forcibly dragged off nearer the North Pole, nearly to the end of the world.

'And don't believe, as you once wrote to me, that I'm trying to put to build up a romance from a distance (this isn't what you wrote, but the meaning is more or less the same). No, I'm as far from romance as the Northern night surrounding me at the moment, as the Yenisei river bearing blocks of ice on its steel back, as the star-spangled sky holding the icy earth in its pinchers'.

'So ever since mid-October there's been only frost, nothing but frost and cold. We awake amid freezing fog through which barely pierce, at a slight distance from each other, the sun, the moon, and still two or three enormous motionless stars like the one over Bethlehem. It's impossible to breathe, it's not air that we swallow but who knows what alloy from another world that goes right through the chest. We hear something ringing out, and the logs that burn you when we pick them up, and the snow under our feet, and the remote barking of dogs, and your own breathing, and the smoke rising from the chimney. The fog doesn't lift'.

'This winter seems quite simply dreadful, even though I struggle rather valiantly with it [. . .]. I'm fed up with this fifty-degrees-below zero cold, with the vagaries of nature and with the crazed weather, which freeze your body as much as your soul. Each footstep, each sigh, is a battle with the elements . . . It's even impossible to stretch one's legs a bit or to take a few simple breaths of fresh air! To all this can be added the darkness, which I've never been able to bear; it weighs down on me atrociously, be it attired with stars, aurorae boreales and other phantasmagorias. The darkness and the cold, this is Hell, and Orthodox Christians are foolish enough to believe that sinners must necessarily be grilled and boiled there, and no longer lick anything that is hot!'

Who wrote these words in 1950? Marina Tsvetaeva's daughter, Ariane Efron, sent into exile at Turukhansk, in Siberia, very near the Arctic Circle.

Who was she writing to? Boris Pasternak, for whom she seems to harbour a passion hardly less lively than her mother had for the same man.

For one who possesses only the volume of these letters admirably translated into French by Simone Luciani, it's difficult to understand what had been the mistake, if there had been one, that caused Ariane Efron, who seemed converted to the regime in power, to be punished with lifelong exile. This matters little here; hers is just one more case to be added to the prosecutor's file, an additional proof of the hatred of the mind that is inherent to any tyranny. But it's also, to my mind, an impressive example of the force that the experience of a harsh fate can give to language and here, between the Moscow of Mandelstam in 1921 and the Kolyma of Shalamov, the experience of cold. For it's not an exaggeration to claim that Ariane Efron, in these letters equals, if not surpasses, her great interlocutor by the quality of her soul and her language.

The poet Varlam Shalamov, who opposed Stalin's regime, was first arrested at the age of twenty-two, in 1929; he was liberated in 1931, arrested again as a 'counter-revolutionary' in 1937, deported to Siberia, where he remained fourteen years; at last liberated in 1951, he died in 1982, a victim of this period which, as he himself wrote, 'managed to make man forget that he is a human being'.

Here, we're up against a boulder, where the heart of man, stripped bare, beats against the rock; where everything is done to destroy man; but from which that man, as well as a few others, was able to return and speak.

The Kolyma camps were located more or less at the same distance from the Arctic Circle as the small town to which Ariane Efron was relegated. The cold there, when Shalamov measures it, is about ten degrees even more intense; but this isn't the worst. To the harsh cold is added hunger, exhaustion because of hunger, illnesses, hard labour, beatings. I do not wish to repeat, I cannot repeat, these tales. Their language is monotonous, poor, hard like those days of rock and ice. It cannot vibrate, because there's nothing in those climes but extreme harshness and cold; even a smile, a friendship, a hope are no longer possible; nothing but hunger, theft, denouncement, beatings, putrefaction wearing down the living body, the thrashes on what is already almost nothing more than a skeleton.

And worst of all, the more or less gradual deterioration of the soul; as happens, in 'The Quarantine', to Captain Schneider, a well-read German communist reduced to scratching the soles of the feet of a gangster who claims to be unable to sleep without this preliminary ritual.

However, despite this, Shalamov survives; not only survives but also comes back to life with an intact faith in poetic language that he ensures has remained his 'fortress' through the worst. How can one not have confidence in such a witness?

While thinking of those fates linked to each other as if by iron chains, I then remembered Dante's *Inferno*. Similarly, the depths of Hell, the 'sad hole', is a place not of flames but, rather, of the abolition of warmth and light, an absolute cold, a frozen lake in the night, a lake hard as rock:

> At that I turned around and saw before me
> a lake of ice stretching beneath my feet,
> more like a sheet of glass than frozen water . . .

The skulls strike against each other like stones because they're so close to each other in anger, in hatred:

> Wood to wood with iron was never clamped
> so firm! And the two of them like billy-goats
> were butting at each other, mad with anger . . .

And tears would be a last trace of human life, a last chance for salvation as well, the tears themselves having become 'crystal visors'. (All visions which, Dante notes in passing, will have given him, for ever, the horror of frozen water.)

The rare merit will have fallen on our century to bring up to the surface of the real world, with real human beings, the harshest scene ever imagined by an implacable genius.

Is it too beautiful, too reassuring, to quote here, as if it responded too well, in my mind, to Aglaya Yepanchin's laughter and to the mountain torrents of Switzerland, this passage, which, at the very end of *Inferno*, tells how Dante and Virgil found the way out?

> Below somewhere there is a space, as far
> from Beelzebub as the limit of his tomb,
> known not by sight but only by the sound
>
> of a little stream that makes its way down here
> through the hollow of a rock that it has worn,
> gently winding in gradual descent.
>
> My guide and I entered that hidden road
> to make our way back up to the bright world . . .

A very deep mystery lies therein. But sometimes, during a trip that is infinitely easier, I'd even by tempted to say almost trivial, I'll have had the same kind of guide to get me untangled.

To get me 'back to the bright world . . . '

Israel: *Blue Notebook*

18 March 1993, in the Zürich-Tel Aviv airplane.

My neighbour, a seventy-two-year-old German man who has been a widower for three years, is coming from Stuttgart and going to spend a few days in Israel to outwit his solitude. (I don't remember, and I doubt that I encouraged him to tell his secrets, but they weren't long in coming.)

He no longer has any fingers on his left hand. Suddenly he becomes very pale; he asks the stewardess to retrieve from the overhead compartment his tensiometer, which he himself puts on his arm. With no apparent worry or nervousness, he explains that his blood pressure has suddenly dropped because of medication that he has taken: he has just gotten over a heart attack. This brief scene recalls the handicapped man in a wheelchair who came to eat at my table in a tea parlour in Mainz, a few months earlier, and who was also Jewish. The man next to me, barely after the colour has returned to his face, starts singing the praises of what the pioneers have done in Israel. It's as if, for this casual trip, an invisible composer had wanted me to hear, beginning with the overture, two related themes: through the deathly paleness crossing the man's complexion and through his amputated hand—as in Mainz the useless legs of the handicapped man—the unforgettable proximity of the violence to which he was subjected; and the second theme: the pride, no less harshly expressed, of the revenge taken on the experience.

(We'll hear this second theme once again in a less predictable way at the end of the trip, when we visit a kibbutz in the northern part of the country—Kfar Blum—founded in 1943 by Germans and Scandinavians—when our guide, a sort of energetic and convincing head military officer-and-nurse, will have us take the tour in a hurry, from the Olympic swimming pool to the big theatre where the poetry reading will take place in the evening and attract so few people that they'll have to be asked to come onstage so that the audience won't seem sparse. The pioneers' pride is comprehensible; a certain exaggeration in regard to the at-least-apparent lack of interest; and this unpleasant mixture of exaltation and more or less military discipline inherent in every community adventure of this kind.)

It's rather cold. The incessant noise of the cars driving by on the street below our Guest House discourages any vague desire to enjoy the garden. In front of us, the ramparts of the old town of Jerusalem, at the foot of which rosemary bushes cover a slope along which paths meander. We soon of course have a single thought: to enter the old town—even if the organizers of the Poetry Festival, for which we have come, try to dissuade us—and to turn our backs on the modern city with its banks and hotels that are as arrogant as they are ordinary.

Because the evening of our arrival, a Friday, coincides with the beginning of the Sabbath, we won't be able to get in touch, without taking some pains, with our hostess whose apartment, in an ill-lit residential quarter, is hidden away at the end of a garden path: it's impossible, of course, to decipher the names, to telephone, and uncalled-for to ring doorbells. Our hostess, Michal G., has generously translated some of the texts that I'll read. She's a self-confident, elegant, beautiful and rather majestic woman who admires Beckett, quotes Derrida and goes more often than we do to Paris where her husband, a scientist, happens to be at the moment for a meeting of the Académie des Sciences of which he is, I think, a corresponding member. A pioneer's daughter, she has recently converted to the Orthodox Jewish faith; whence the silent telephone and doorbell, the benediction at the meal, the passing of a bowl of white wine from one guest to another. And when, during the evening, she wants me to hear the quite moving recording of Paul Celan reading his poetry in Tel Aviv in 1969, she has to ask her less ritual-oriented friends to plug in the tape recorder—an act that they'll deem, in return, rather hypocritical.

For us, there's something strange about discovering as coexistent in the same person a culture, tastes and even a language that are entirely 'modern'—too 'modern', to my mind—and this conversion, apparently without the slightest qualms, to a ritualism more than a thousand years old.

(I'll see Michal G. two years later, during a television show devoted to Jerusalem and filmed just above our Guest House back then, across from the old town whose lights would come on with nightfall. With her, religious figures: a young rabbi, a Christian Palestinian priest, a French archaeologist who was also a priest, and a single 'real' Palestinian who had come there, as he said, without being authorized by the Israeli police and who was rather awkwardly, even if legitimately, aggressive; but the theological, lyrical or symbolical remarks of the other guests—Michal G. compared the Holy City to female genitals without her logic, at the time, seeming very clear to me— seemed to float a little too high above the ordinary, brutal realities of which the Palestinian was the painful insistent reminder and to whom no one was apparently very concerned about listening.)

Lev Berinsky, one of the poets whom we have met here and one of the rare poets who writes in Yiddish: born in Bessarabia, which was Romanian at the time, he was saved, in 1939, by the Red Army, who took him to the USSR. He'll live for thirty years in Moscow, where he'll end up abandoning his flat and taking refuge in Israel, with all this family. He lives in Akka, in obviously difficult material conditions. He has translated Rilke and Chagall's poems, which creates at least a literary link between us. He's a rather frail, bearded man with a humble and painful look in his eyes, as has been seen much too often in much too many images of persecution.

(The scenes of the Passion: whipping, spitting, insults . . . Where have we seen this in contemporary reality when it's not, horribly, in images of pogroms doomed to 'cleanse' Germany of its Jewish 'vermin'?)

Beginning with the morning of the second day, I much liked the little valley that opens up at the base of the Mishkenot Guest House: a grassy hollow on a slope with a few white stone steps in a semi-circle similar to the vestiges of an amphitheatre; although it offers a sort of haven just above the busy road below, it attracted few strollers. The only time that we walked across it, a young Arab or Israeli boy was riding his horse with an elegant casualness; two ladies were sitting on the stone steps and looking at a city map. That horse and its rider, in this place, didn't seem entirely real—with no links to the rest of the world and the noisy events of the day.

The first time that we ventured into the old town, and as the tiny streets of the Arab quarter became emptier as we approached the mosques, which were in fact inaccessible during those days, we ended up feeling— perhaps especially because of our hosts' warnings— some anxiety. We could also have felt anxiety on another day because, on the contrary, of the crowds pressing into the same quarters: Muslims whose heads were covered with their chequered *keffiyehs* as they left the mosques, Christian pilgrims bending beneath a heavy cross in the labyrinth of the Via Dolorsa, while in the middle of the Arab quarter, across from a small synagogue maintained there as if defiantly, Israeli flags were emblazoning a balcony; and always, more or less everywhere, armed soldiers on guard; and weapons as well—plastic weapons—in the hands of almost all the little Arabs. We cannot walk in these streets as simple travellers, as we've done so often in Paris, in Rome, as we'd do (but I'm not so sure, now that we've gone there) in Moscow, or even in Cairo or Fez. We're in a place that is too odd, like a cave where, for centuries, religious alcohols which were admirably strong and pure at the origin have been made but from which, after fermentation, would now ultimately emanate only dangerous miasmas. As a result, we can no longer be simple strollers in quest of past beauty and truth, of present vitality. The proximity to violence makes us see more in relief, or in another kind of relief; we imagine, but it's mostly an illusion, that we're closer to reality, more involved in the present, even if it's because of that slight risk that we—as we'd been informed—would take by coming here.

Here we are in the Church of the Holy Sepulchre. During his visit in 1806, Chateaubriand writes: 'I remained for more than a half hour on my knees in the little room of the Holy Sepulchre, everyone staring at the stone without being able to look away'; and further on: 'The Church of the Holy Sepulchre, which consists of several churches, built on uneven ground, lit by a multitude of lamps, is oddly mysterious: a darkness favourable to piety and the meditation of the soul reigns. The Christian priests of the different sects live in the different parts of the building. From the top of the arcades, where they nest like doves, from the depths of the chapels and underground passages, they let their canticles resound at all hours of the day and night: the Roman Catholic monk's organ, the Abyssinian priest's cymbals, the Greek caloyer's voice, the solitary Armenian's prayer, and the Copt monk's lament knock in turn at the door of your ear; you don't know where these concerts are coming from; you breathe the fragrant incense without glimpsing the hand burning it: yet you see going by, disappearing behind columns, and vanishing into the shadows of the temple, the pontiff who is going to celebrate the most redoubtable of mysteries in the same places where they took place.' Of course, I entered this same place, more than two centuries later, without this believer's faith; all the same, I'd also been raised in the Christian religion, albeit in its Protestant form, and the Passion had been rendered sufficiently present to me first through the Gospels, then through art—so many masterpieces, and so different—and especially through Bach's music, so that the visit of such a sanctuary couldn't leave me indifferent. (All the more so in that I don't consider myself to have an irreligious temperament.) But the least one can say is that 'a darkness favourable to piety and the meditation of the soul' now longer reigns: the vain curiosity of the tourists, too many wherever they are, and the stupider, it would seem, as their numbers increase, the fanatical or inane exaltation of many of the pilgrims, and the coexistence, which is hardly peaceful, as one knows, of various religious currents which watch over the Holy Places, give you vertigo instead of any sentiment of fervour and veneration.

At the entrance, a woman, moving her hands with extraordinary speed, sets down some small pebbles among the quickly faded flowers tossed down as an offering on the Stone of Unction (where the body of Christ, having been brought down from the cross, was supposedly anointed with a mixture of myrrh and aloe)—a beautiful rose limestone slab above which a row of suspended lamps makes one think of Japanese lanterns—and then takes back the pebbles: she has made herself some relics in this way. She looks like someone writing, then just as soon erasing her message, in haste, as if she feared that it would be deciphered over her shoulder. In such gestures, as in those chanced upon in other sanctuaries when pilgrims touch statues with their hands or lips, there's the same, seemingly feverish, seemingly furtive haste, which sometimes possesses something almost obscene. (I suddenly think of those extraordinary agile croupiers who take in all the bets on the gambling tables. But here, one will have pocketed a few invisible coins to feel a little less destitute in regard to a harsh destiny.)

On the back of the Holy Sepulchre of Christ, the Copts are entitled to a very small chapel draped in pink (or so I recall it). A monk with a delicate, emaciated face framed by a black hood, as a country girl might have worn in winter in the old days, invites us with his benign voice to enter so that he can show us a part of the 'real grave'—which implies that the other grave, in front of which so many pilgrims have marched in procession for centuries, is false—and to offer us, with a pious image, a very small crucifix. This exiguous niche resembled the tiny booth of a fortune-teller in a fair. Across the way, the dark chapel of the Syrians where an altar that has lost its gilt—its only ornamentation—is falling apart, provides an access to the grave of Joseph of Arimathea. A squad of Czech pilgrims are following their guide's explanations: a woman feverishly shakes our hands in passing, her eyes full of tears.

Armenian monks are officiating in the central nave, the 'katholikon', which is set apart for them. One of them, standing in the centre in front of the iconostasis, is delivering a long and seemingly vehement homily. On the sides, other monks and a few women dressed in black; no music, no singing. When they come back out after the service, they're in a procession, preceded by two attendants wearing a red fez and each equipped with a heavy, silver knobbed cane with which they imperiously strike the ground. However, I come across one of the monks, who has stepped out of the ranks and is using a very long metal tube—which terminates on its lower end with a rubber squeezer—to extinguish the candles one by one, aiming this curious extinguisher at the head of an elderly lady parishioner and blowing a little breeze into her hair. Periods of time thus blend strangely, like moods: formal or playful, solemn or frenetic. We're more disconcerted than moved because of this.

The same is true in the chapel of Calvary, where too much flashiness clutters up a place that cannot be imagined except as stripped bare—this place so appropriately named 'skull'—and as located outside the city, between ground ready to tremble and a stormy sky. It's better to leave as soon as possible these souks of curiosity and superstition.

Thanks to a well-advised guide, an Italian from Cuneo whose family, Jewish of course, probably originated from Cavaillon, we climbed up to the roof of an building next to the Holy Sepulchre, a concrete terrace in a corner of which a few wretched alveoli must be used as cells by Abyssinian monks: a sort of henhouse set down on the greyish roof. One of these monks, who is still young, bearded as they all are, and very dark-skinned, was sitting there in full sunlight, on a tottering chair, with some vague book in his hands. He emerged from his lethargy only reluctantly when asked by our guide to lead us to the chapel, one floor below: a small modest chapel one of whose walls is decorated with a panel of naively coloured images representing the story of Solomon and the Queen of Sheba, from whom, according to tradition, a part of the Ethiopian people are descendants. Another monk, apparently very old, was the only person there: sitting completely at the back, absolutely motionless as if centuries had passed over him without altering him or even making him move; it seems to me that his clothing—or was it cloth draped behind him?—had intense and straightforward colours like those of their evangelistaries.

Suddenly that place, with so few visitors despite the proximity of the Holy Sepulchre, and those two monks, struck me as being hardly real: as if they'd been forgotten by history and subsisted on its margins, almost similar to the figurines of nativity scenes; moreover, they were saying nothing; and I don't believe that we'd have had the idea of uttering the slightest word to them. Even today, as I find them engraved in my memory, I wonder what their thoughts might have been, and if it's conceivable that they'd kept their faith alive inside them, sheltered by their silence and immobility. I especially wondered about this for the monk whom we aroused from his somnolence on the grey concrete terrace: What sort of life subsisted in him? While remaining next to him as we did for a while, we didn't attribute much more life to him than to an animal of a rather slow species such as a tortoise or a woodlouse; but this was perhaps unfair.

The question implied by this astonishment, at that moment, is the following: Can human beings placed in similar conditions harbour a real, living faith—or aren't they indeed no longer but nativity scene figurines ossified in traditional religious scenes for a more or less respectful, more or less indifferent public?

They seemed to be in exile—rather like those melancholy wild animals of zoos—in a climate that is indeed not theirs; and in addition, they're obviously not very numerous, like an endangered species that no one cares about protecting. Can the awareness of being elected to live out their entire lives next to Christ's grave, to be, as it were, the guardians of it along with others who are cut off a little less from the world, like the Armenians, suffice for ensuring their inner plenitude? What would one find in their heads, if one could go into them for a moment? Obsessions of wild animals or, more probably, at the end, a vague darkness?

It will be said that this question can be raised for all people belonging to a religious order who are shut away, who still subsist in our world at the end of the second millennium after the birth of Christ. All the same: if it's certain that among them are human beings whose faith has wavered, felt threatened or burnt-out, leaving them with a painful sense of emptiness, the few whom we manage to glimpse in such-and-such a circumstance, nearer to us, have never appeared as abandoned to themselves, as disinherited. Nor in Israel, those who live in a monastery on the slope of a valley like birds nesting in a cliff; because it then seems to us, rightly or wrongly, that there, the open space, and the black column of a cypress perhaps indicating a source, must be of sufficient aid for the solitude; as if, at the end, the outdoors, the sound of water, even the almost imperceptible sound of the sand announcing the desert were so many words ready to weave themselves into another form of prayer, which wouldn't enter into competition with real prayer, but which would, instead, amplify it, like a response.

(Even as what I saw in Israel during those few days, made undoubtedly more striking and serious because of the tension reigning nearly everywhere, because of the justified feeling that an explosion could take place at any moment, someone scream, lose his or her blood, collapse—what I saw, glimpsed, thought I saw there, as far as religion is concerned, made me experience once again contradictory and thus disconcerting emotions—as if the best and the worst persistently subsisted side by side—with, to be truthful, the worst being predominant: that is, more or less pathetic superstition, and ever-frightening fanaticism.)

An example? Provided that one arrives early enough, and the group isn't too big, it's possible to attend some of the Armenian services at the Cathedral of Saint James, a twelfth-century church shaped like a cross. It's one of the most beautiful churches in the city, and in front of it extends a rectangular courtyard as simple as it is austere. There, a tall monk dressed in a long black robe was holding open a heavy rose-coloured curtain to let the officiating priests enter. Instead of bells, heavy wooden or bronze bar-like gongs, which hang in the entryway, are struck.

To our left, from a sort of loggia looming over a door doubtless leading to the sacristy, a young monk was reading aloud from a very big book. Facing us were three side chapels: a golden-yellow cloth with some kind of bright red geometrical pattern was hanging across the one on the left. All of a sudden, a group of children, noisy as if at the end of a school day, headed across the nave towards the sacristy, from which they emerged almost as soon, incomprehensibly wearing surplices whose admirable colours were rather muted. Monks kept entering; some of them, probably belonging to a higher rank, were wearing on their head a hood which, seen from behind, formed a high black triangle. The children gathered in the side chapel on the right, the older monks in the one to the left; and from one chapel to the other one, very beautiful songs responded to each other. Oil lamps were sizzling above our heads.

I can't content myself with noting down impressions so barely rational and so contradictory, at least in appearance, as these, without trying to understand them.

What emerges from my memory of the Armenian service is that the church itself, the sacerdotal vestments and the liturgy immediately seemed 'beautiful', that is, formed a coherent, harmonious ensemble, creating a sentiment of plenitude, as if they'd nonetheless retained a kind of meaning, even for us. Moreover, since the monks were relatively numerous and since the children, also numerous, had joined them, the coherence of the ritual increased, as it were, and above all was revitalized—all the more so in that the children were not pallid novices forcefully removed from the world. We'd watched them entering as a still-turbulent group, having just escaped from school or been taken from their games on one of those squares whose luminous quietude, compared to the feverishness of the overpopulated narrow streets elsewhere, had indeed also touched us.

What could thus be the sense of all this? Hadn't we merely experienced a purely esthetical emotion, even as we might have been convinced by one play at a theatre and not by another one, because of the quality of the writing, the staging, or the actors? Perhaps this was somewhat the case, provided it's not forgotten that, in my opinion, a theatre play capable of affecting me in such a way would necessarily have made me glimpse or recover a kind of deep truth even if I didn't know the language, even if I knew all too well the subject matter—as had been the case for this Armenian service.

I'll thus have seen or glimpsed during those few days, concentrated in that place more umbilical for us, in any event, than Delphi, and put into relief—let me insist upon the fact—by a state of latent war and by the impassioned violence of the circumstances, very diverse and sometimes mutually incompatible signs of the sacred: some of the signs pathetic or even distressing, because on them the long wearing down of past time had completely tarnished and dulled the force and the vitality of the original event, had domesticated, vulgarized and debased it; the other signs disturbing or worse, because that original violence—the whip raised against the merchants of the Temple, for instance, but also the threats and promises of the Prophets—had not waned but had congealed and coagulated into rituals that had become blind, knotted like a knot of darkness that no longer had any possibility of being untied except through a kind of violence no longer 'pure' like the violence at the origin, but corrupted through its too long fermentation and ready for the worst explosions.

(The day after the day when, two and a half years after the trip, I'd jotted down these thoughts, Yitzhak Rabin was assassinated by a Jewish student.)

Upon leaving the Church of the Holy Sepulchre, we stopped to eat a pita accompanied by a glass of orange juice outdoors, next to the market of Muristan in the tepid sunlight of that 22nd March. It's a part of the Christian quarter about which the *Blue Guide*, my only reference as I transcribe these notes, rather oddly utters not a single word. A sort of vast rectangular market square with a fountain in the middle and surrounded by buildings which were perhaps Ottoman in style and whose beautifully coloured stones were harmoniously arranged. One would almost believe oneself transported into an Italian town; and this deserted area, after leaving behind the souks and the Church of the Holy Sepulchre also invaded by the crowd, creates an impression of respite. And it's also somewhat as though the eight-line stanzas of *Jerusalem Delivered* were being recited between two hostile and more or less degenerated liturgies. 'The Combat of Tancred and Clorinda': were I a theatre director, this is where I'd like to stage and make the admirable poem resound, more than at the base of the ramparts. But in any event, how far this fable, only the enveloping sensuality of which still moves us today, would seem from the Bible and the Quran!

The Church of Saint-Anne, built in the twelfth century in a very pure style, in memory of the parents of the Virgin who lived in the quarter, stands at the very end or, rather, at the beginning—for we're walking in the opposite direction—of the Via Dolorosa, a few big cobblestones of which are still visible. It's a street lined with little shops and invaded by passers-by and detritus. Right alongside is the pool called 'probatic' (was it because of sheep prepared for sacrifices there?), dug not far from a Roman sanctuary devoted to Asclepius. In the Gospel of John (5: 2–4), one reads: 'Now there is at Jerusalem by the sheep market a pool, which is called in the Hebrew tongue Bethesda, having five porches. [They have been found.] In these porches lay a great multitude of impotent folk, the blind, halt, withered, waiting for the moving of the water. For an angel went down at a certain season into the pool, and troubled the water: whosoever then first after the troubling of the water stepped in was made whole of whatsoever disease he had.' While I was contemplating with emotion these excavations and in order to remove myself from the passing crowd, it was not this passage that I recalled but, rather, Rimbaud's never-forgotten poem: 'Bethseda, the pool of five porches, was where trouble could occur. It seemed to be a sinister washing place, ever burdened with rain and darkness, with beggars stirring on its inside steps illuminated by gleams of storms announcing hellish lightning to come and joking about their blind blue eyes or about the blue or white cloth wrapped around their stumps. O military laundry house, O public baths! The water was always black, and no cripple ever fell into it, even in a dream'. No less than these resurgences of myth and history in poetry and music are needed to restore genuine life to ruins and sites whose meaning vanishes little by little, worn down by time and by the hebetude of the ever-more numerous eyes which, moreover, much less look at than merely graze them. (I'd thus be tempted to write that never, anywhere, the event of Christ's death will have more deeply penetrated me than when listening to the singing in one or the other of Bach's *Passions*; or even, all the same, while thinking more about this, in Hölderlin's ingenuous élan towards this last god of the gods: ' . . . But the observant man / saw God's face / back then, there, at the mystery of the grapevine / when they were sitting together at the Last Supper, / and in the great soul of the Lord, having chosen and foretold His own death, / and His last love, / for never enough could He speak of goodness, / nor affirm what affirms. But his light was death. / For mean is the anger of the world. / But he knew this. All is good. Then he died. / But his friends, however, could contemplate / one last time the shape of He who renounced, / bent over before God as when a century bows down, thoughtfully, / in the joy of truth, / / and they became sad as evening / now had come. Indeed remaining pure / before such a face is a fate, a life that has a heart, and it lasts more than a half . . . '

In front of the Wailing Wall, which is a fragment of the retaining wall of the Western Wall of the destroyed Temple: those great old stones are ochre as if worn down by the centuries-long prayers and tears of the Jews. Here, as in other holy places of Judaism, as in the surf that is suggested by the gravestones of the cemetery of Prague and that makes one think of Caspar David Friedrich's *Shipwreck*, you're gripped by respect, as if weighing down over you were all the suffering that has been, for so many centuries, the fate of this 'chosen' people. Nevertheless, you look on with unaccustomed, perhaps naive eyes, in any case eyes without prejudices (be they favourable ones or not); and what you see is frightening: all those men dressed in black with their broad-rimmed hats, with their little braids, showing their pale complexions; and the ungraspable looks of those seminarians, groups of whom one sometimes used to come across in the streets long ago, inspire the same feelings, perhaps of pity, certainly of remoteness. One of them, still young and rather skinny, with his big golden-buckled shoes, his pant legs knotted below his knees, his long hat, and with the pile of holy books that he was carrying under his arm, made me think of Basilio as he's sometimes represented in stagings of *The Marriage of Figaro*. He kept twirling like a feverish man between the Wailing Wall, the toilets and the Office of the Rabbi of the Wailing Wall.

Another man facing the Wall didn't content himself with nodding his head rhythmically as they all do; sometimes he violently stamped on the ground, as one stamps one's feet in anger, with a white, naked foot in his big black shoe.

I couldn't help but have the impression that a kind of insanity was taking place there, one that was more worrisome than respectable; as if a blind, savage ritual, with its back turned to the world, were being perpetuated in front of those stones; and without my being able to imagine any divine face in front of those men, a face whose reflection would have warmed them by softening their own facial features. I'm not forgetting that I was watching all this from the outside; indeed from the outside, since I couldn't watch in any other way a ritual that struck me as funereal and threatening.

(Basically, it was as if there were no single wall on this square but, rather, four, between which men dressed in black had shut themselves up as in a fortress that they're doubtless ready to defend until the very last one of them has died. How could a belief that shuts one in still have something to do with supernatural light?)

In chilly greyish weather, we head for the Mount of Olives and begin by visiting, at the bottom, the Church of the Tomb of the Virgin Mary. One needs to go down a long staircase that vanishes towards the crypt under a trellis of suspended lamps (the church is Greek Orthodox). In front of the stone of the tomb, candles sputter like crickets in summer. An emotion comes to you, nevertheless, however remote you are from what could be no more than theatre for most of us; it's because of all those stair steps that we followed underground, as in so many folk tales, especially the one about Aladdin, never forgotten since childhood; because of the bond that is made there between the rock, the event of a death and the flame burning even inside this kind of cavern. It matters little that this place is, or is not, that of a legend: it's no less than as if, while going down those stair steps, we'd come closer to something like a dark truth that imposes silence upon us for a few moments; the nervous, flickering flame of the candles seems to reach the stone; and perhaps as well, without our being aware of it at the time, these words rise inside us: 'Mary, mother of God', acting like an oil on the stone, on the very stone that our heart, in time, is threatened to become. Such are knots in the mind that have the particularity of tying together, and untying, everything.

At the exit, little Palestinian children sell stacks of more or less shop-spoiled postcards, held together by rubber bands, which we buy more willingly than any relic.

The Garden of Olives, on the other hand, is pampered like the main square of a small provincial town, where the very inauthentic Church of All Nations was built, at the beginning of this century, around a rock on which Christ had supposedly prayed: it's impossible to feel or imagine anything there, whence one single desire: to leave without waiting any more.

(This is what I noted on the spot in my blue notebook. It's impossible to leave this as it is, when at stake is an event whose shadow—and light—has extended over so many souls, all the way to our day. But it's true that what is offered to us here are 'pious images' like those that used to be slipped into communicants' missals, the watering down by all possible means of what was sorrow and anguish 'until death', infinite solitude and the sweating of blood. Beneath the leaves of the olive trees which grow among the rocks, and which shelter no one from that evil, but which had the same density of reality as that evil; whereas those little gravel paths, those little flowers in the flowerbeds and all the labelling that follows are mere illusions that make everything dwarf-size.)

We're almost at the summit. An Arab who is selling postcards and overhears us speaking French, violently inveighs against Mitterrand and France as if he were spitting on our shoes.

Below us extends the vast Jewish necropolis that was ravaged between 1949 and 1967: a uniformly grey colour beneath a sky that is iron grey today; many tombs gaping open, with their covers shattered or toppled over (as can be seen in certain representations of the Last Judgement); an almost rubbish-dump-like appearance; with here and there rusted braziers on which visitors make fires, like tramps.

Jews apparently had themselves buried here to conform to the prophecies of Zechariah, whose supposed tomb can be visited where it lies halfway up the slope and in the middle of a filthy farm courtyard in which poultry roam between time-worn chicken-wire fencing; prophecies that situate, in this place, the Resurrection of the dead on the Last Judgement Day. But to block their path, Muslims have installed their sepulchres just across the way, at the foot of the ramparts and the Golden Gate. On the grassy terraces, beneath the trees, a few graves are indeed still scattered as if they formed a herd that had been grazing, motionless, for centuries. Here, as always, grass gets on well with graves; it appeases them, almost tenderly absorbs them.

Between the Temple Mount and the Mount of Olives extends Kidron Valley. Why has this place name seemed familiar to me for so long? It must be mere reverie. The torrent that used to sweep along, and purify, the ashes or the dust of the destroyed idols has no longer flowed, except on rare occasions, for a long time. One sees sparse vegetation, blinding dust, grey and ochre boulders from which have been carved porticos, pillars, rooms, as in Petra, though more modestly; and as in Petra, even if one had seen this site only in photos, one would be moved by the elegance, the refinement, imposed upon the roughest and wildest land that the earth can offer. A little to the wayside of these supposed tombs of the prophets rises 'Absalom's pillar', a Hellenistic funereal monument capped with a stone cone evoking the various ways hair was done up in the ancient Middle East.

Absalom: David's rebellious son, the handsome young man whose hair was so thick it was shaved off every year and weighed 200 shekels, that is, more than 2 kilos; it cost him his life one day in battle when it got caught in the branches of an oak tree and one of David's officers, spotting the trapped rebel, thrust three darts through his heart. Absalom: both a name and an image, of this same death, which have stayed with me ever since childhood, among many other images because, like most European children, I was nourished with them very early on: the dove of the Ark, Moses saved from the river and then rediscovered later in Poussin's great calm paintings, Moses on Mount Sinai, Joseph deciphering dreams in Egypt— there would be too many stories to mention whose effects on us were so bizarre, given that our own lifestyle had so few similarities to that of the Hebrews, the Philistines, or the Egyptians, even as our climates and landscapes had so little to do with theirs.

The Kidron Valley and the so-called Absalom's Monument: Paul Celan mentions them in one of his last poems, because his brief stay in Israel preceded his death. I've qualms about speaking about it here, where I'm gathering only quick, superficial notes, whereas in Celan's poetic *oeuvre* every word is so dense, and the tension so great, since everything seems heading towards its end. In the blazing heat (that can easily be imagined in this valley without the slightest shade), there's nothing more than the mere braying of a donkey, which is there in the 'reality' of the moment but which comes from further back, from the very depths of the Old Testament (more than from the New Testament, which is rejected here, bypassed—Gethsemane, Christ's cavalry, indeed bypassed for the 'tomb' of Absalom): 'Now Absalom in his lifetime had taken up and reared up for himself a pillar, which is in the king's dale: for he said, I have no son to keep my name in remembrance'; for Celan, this is the only thing, and the gates of the town, the walled-in gate—and the last gate, the only open one, is that of the beloved woman accompanying him, in this end of all time, when the star itself is seen as 'keeled over', 'beswamped' . . .

(A sort of embarrassment, therefore, could keep me from continuing to speak: I haven't a single deep root in these places, even if it's here that has blossomed in a very mysterious way a spiritual space that will have been ours, whatever faith we have, and even if many of us have never adhered to it with faith. I've seen only from afar, in images, the grey hell of the camps; none of my close friends died in them and I don't wish to mimic anything, especially where suffering is concerned; no ordeal up to now has been harsh enough to make words stick in my throat, as happened to Paul Celan. All the same, it mustn't be forgotten any more that facing you, coming nearer and nearer every day, almost at hand's reach, is what will make you stop speaking once and for all. But perhaps, until the end, an abyss remains between what has been experienced and what will be experienced, even if a very great share of what is experienced, the past, seems to have escaped us and is thus no more than fumes as inconsistent as dreams or the future; despite this, it seems to me that many traces of experience are still present for us, and sometimes more or less visibly active, in the folds of our bodies and deeper within; and that, consequently, we still possess them, like a burden or a treasure for ourselves. It's better to refrain from speaking about what is to come because, even if it's foreseeable, it belongs to the realm of the fumes: what hasn't yet been experienced. Even here, therefore, where I get close to abysses without taking any risks, the only rule to impose upon myself would be to speak in accordance with my nature and experience; or to say nothing any more. To speak 'de Profundis', one must have gone down into the depths; to speak about borders, one must have been deported, or have run the risk of crossing them.)

The Temple Platform. At last arriving on this esplanade that had remained closed to non-Muslims until the end of our stay, I was even more ignorant than in other places to which, at least, were attached remote images and sometimes more than that. I'll nonetheless express, naively, what I felt there. As we were climbing the large, gently rising steps leading to the esplanade, I felt for the first time in Jerusalem a sensation of happiness, of alleviation, of openness: because of those svelte arches that rose in front of us and, here and there, farther on, on the terrace, because of their elegance and uselessness, an appearance of freedom in the way the small domed monuments that surround the Grand Al-Aqsa Mosque had been laid out, and all this with a dazzling whiteness in broad sunlight. I didn't know whatsoever what all the monuments and their layout corresponded to, but I'm not sure that knowledge is the essential thing here. A simple postcard, an offhand view of the esplanade, refreshes my memory today. There are very few people around the Mosque, just a few figurines in shadows so short that it must be midday, figurines making one think of pawns on a chessboard (but without black squares); who also evoke Giorgio de Chirico's 'metaphysical' town squares. There, it's not the blue and gold Grand Mosque that retains my attention, although it dominates everything; it's the secondary elements made of white stone like the esplanade and laid out according to a rule which escapes me (and which could, in fact, not exist). I believe that I'm thinking of the desert and of constructions that would blend with it to better preserve shade in them, and the water of a fountain. Moreover, with its arches as if freely standing there, floral, almost weightless (which, for a moment, make the admirable temple of Segesta, not to mention those of Karnak, appear so solemn, so massive, in memory), I sense what can also be so graceful and extremely refined in that Islam of which we risk seeing today, because of its extremists, only the dark violence—a violence that joins, in a collision of wounds and tears, that of the fanatics of the Western Wall, champing at the bit in their impatience for a definitive triumph of Israel.

I didn't have to know the tradition according to which Muhammad had taken flight here, towards heaven, for this esplanade to seem to be a take-off area.

If you wish to go to Bethlehem, you need to find an Arab taxi driver. This can easily be done at the Jaffa Gate. Ours is named Ibrahim; he's taking advantage of the opportunity to have an old friend sit down, next to him, who claims that he also needs to go there, but who, from all appearances, will only be offering himself a free ride. Once the driver arrives in Bethlehem, he'll buy a big cake for his daughter's birthday.

He takes an old road winding through a landscape of stones, olive trees, goat herds, and with fewer modern buildings than elsewhere. But wherever we go here, we're far from pastorals. At a given moment, the taxi drives through a miserable small town where the potholed road becomes barely practicable and all of whose walls are covered with red or black inscriptions obviously aimed against Israel and, in any case, aggressive in their colours and the way they've been written: brute expressionism. Blood and sweat, blood and mourning.

Bethlehem is an ordinary-looking town. The Israeli police station, which stands across from the

Church of the Nativity, is protected by a high trellis. One is as far as possible from any 'Good News'; and even if the severe architecture of the basilica is beautiful, even if there are few visitors because the tension reigning in these zones keeps them away, one feels less moved here than at the Holy Sepulchre. The effort needed to join up with the original mystery of the birth of Christ is too great; the brutality of the present prohibits access to it; this obstacle is much graver than the small size of the door that forces the visitor to stoop to enter.

Heading for the northern part of the country, we make a stopover on Mount Gilboa, a Biblical site where bright flowers, some of which are very rare, as we're told, grow among stones as numerous as they are. The sun is also at its brightest. This is where Saul's great battle against the Philistines was waged, and where his defeat, his death as well as Jonathan's took place. And it's on the ramparts of Beth-Shan, whose ruins, going back to the Roman period, we've just visited, that the vanquishing Philistines nailed their corpses.

When he learnt of the defeat, David cursed the mountains where we are: 'Ye mountains of Gilboa, let there be no dew, neither let there be rain, upon you, nor fields of offerings: for there the shield of the mighty is vilely cast away, the shield of Saul, as though he had not been anointed with oil.' And he deplores the death of his friend: 'I am distressed for thee, my brother Jonathan: very pleasant hast thou been unto me: thy love to me was wonderful, passing the love of women.'

The young man who reads this lamentation to us seems made to put all the necessary passion into it. But at least as far as the dew and the rain are concerned, the malediction has long been lifted.

The story of the death of Saul who, seeing that he was defeated, asks an Amalekite soldier to kill him, upon which this soldier, who announces Saul's death to David, is himself slain: this story, and the corpses nailed to the ramparts of Beth-Shan, under athe bright sun 'shining on the just and the unjust', reminds us that violence doesn't date from yesterday, and that the Old Testament, which impregnated our childhood, offers many encouraging examples to the current intransigence of Israel. Ever since that very ancient book, and the other ancient books, those epic tales which have not without reason taken on the sense of 'war stories' for our minds, even if the etymology by no means makes this necessary, war has never stopped sparking up here and there on the globe, exactly as savagely today as on the very first day. This irremediable evil obsesses us; perhaps we see less and less what can oppose it; perhaps we're at a moment in history when there are more open wounds than threads to stitch them back together.

The Jordan River is but a trickle of brownish water; most of the time, its course can be located only because of the trees bordering it and hiding it. (But what a path its waters have made in us, all the same, ever since Christ was baptized in them by John the Baptist and, after he'd come 'straightway out of the water', saw the Holy Spirit descending like a dove on him! One cannot act as if this didn't take place; nor, later, the encounter at Emmaus . . .)

Today, Lake Tiberias is dull, like most lakes, depending on the light falling upon them. Fishermen are no longer found on the shore where we make a halt, only swimmers; and on the site where the miracle of the multiplication of the loaves took place, a silly new church has been built around a bit of exposed rocky ground. However, if we climbed one day to the grassy heights that dominate the lake (and where we'd have much trouble seeing someone walking on the water), perhaps we'd encounter one of those 'little blue nuns' who sometimes make a retreat there when they're not helping the poor and sickly in Jerusalem. They're mostly old women who are both intelligent and naive, serious and capable of bursting out in laughter like schoolgirls over a trifle, and who wouldn't be here, and wouldn't be who they are, without that dove over the Jordan River and those footsteps on the water of a little lake in the Near East.

Towards the desert. We go down the Wadi Qelt valley, nourished with water sources that seem to be as many miracles in these arid hills, towards the Monastery of Saint George of Choziba. (As we go past camps of Bedouins with big black tents, our Jewish guide, who is nevertheless well-informed, mocks the claim of these nomads 'without hearth or home' to defend their land: he reminds me of that young French Protestant, coming back home from the Algerian War, who would contemptuously say of the local population: 'They don't even know how to knot a tie!')

A cypress tree inhabited by chirping birds indicates the beginning of a trail going up to the monastery; there, more birds, cats, young monks and, a little higher than the church, caves where, as we're told, hermits sometimes make a retreat like birds in cliffs. Here it seems to me—but isn't this once again an illusion based on so little?—that the chirping and the noise, down below, of water defying stone and sand, can help the ancient Word, which brings together these few people here, to retain a little truth of a lustral, thirst-quenching power.

(We won't see, further down, near Jericho, the Monastery of Temptation: our driver, an Ukrainian Jew who has arrived only recently in Israel, refuses to remain alone and wait for us on the parking lot next to the archaeological digs, fearing that he'll be singled out and taken to task.)

When one looks out towards Jordan, the land of the Moabites, and the other shore of the Dead Sea from the citadel of Masada, one has the impression of gazing—through the furnace-like heat—at the lower part of a city with a bare, modern, seemingly crystalline kind of architecture, where in fact stand only pale sand formations (this is where, across from this kind of bottleneck, that the Dead Sea seems split in two). When we come back at the end of the afternoon, the mountains, higher up, towards the north, will have taken on little by little an ivory and vaguely rose colour, the appearance of a substance that isn't hazy like mist, but—I cannot put it otherwise— immaterial. It's on the slope of one of these mountains that Moses is supposed to have stopped in order to greet the Promised Land before he died and was buried, doubtless too tall for any grave, in a place whose whereabouts are unknown: 'but no man knoweth of his sepulchre unto this day.'

In Qumran, while I was looking at the openings of caves dug into the cliffs which resemble gigantic elephant feet, it seemed to me that I was still hearing the noise of a ceramic pot hit by the stones that Bedouin shepherds had thrown while looking for a lost sheep, just as in the Bible; and who found there, if not their ewe, then the manuscripts of the Essenes.

Biblical words seem to recover all their meaning in such places which haven't changed over the centuries, where there are nearly only stones and a few birds, and salt-thickened water, where no signposts and educational panels yet exist, where even what has been brought along by our times is more or less mere rusted iron and crumbled walls, or a makeshift booth from which a little fruit is sold, where what is elementary has still not let its violence be domesticated. 'He looked towards Sodom and Gomorrah, and towards all the land of the plain, and beheld, and, lo, the smoke of the country went up as the smoke of a furnace': Sodom and Gomorrah were near where we are; and, in this very arid place, a rain of 'brimstone and fire' wouldn't have surprised us, even today. Here, we learn once again what dust is, that wind can be blinding, that stones split. We understand the God who is equated, in Isaiah, to 'a clear heat upon herbs, and like a cloud of dew in the heat of harvest'.

All this hangs together, is consonant: the sand, the ground at the bottom of the Dead Sea, the noise of a stone against a ceramic pot hidden in a cave, the herds of goats or sheep in sparse grass; but also what has been found in the caves and which can now been seen in the Shrine of the Book in Jerusalem: those sandals worn by soldiers, those baskets woven of straw, those fragments of letters on papyrus which were written by an insurgent Jewish general to his officers and whose Hebrew characters are shaped like iron tools. All this bears witness to a harmony henceforth almost entirely broken between man and the most naked and necessary elements of the world in which he lives. But I've found nothing more, on the edge of the Dead Sea, than the very old and strong nostalgia for the archaic, for what is original, that which makes Aeschylus—already to Hugo and then to Claudel—seem greater than Euripides, that *The Illiad*, to our worn eyes, surpasses the poetry of Theocritus, that Segesta in its mountains appears the most venerable of the Greek temples of Sicily, equal, as it were, to the mountains surrounding it, and that Vézelay also inspires more reverence in us than later cathedrals, however beautiful their architecture might be. Sites which, first and foremost, impose silence.

But we mustn't then forget the cruelty, the implacability that reigned in those worlds, the God of Moses saying 'I will make mine arrows drunk with blood', General Sisera killed in his sleep by a woman who hammers a tent nail into the temple of his skull, Delilah putting out Samson's eyes, or that story told at the end of the nineteenth chapter of Judges, and that I'd like to quote in its entirety:

> And, behold, there came an old man from his work out of the field at even, which was also of mount Ephraim; and he sojourned in Gibeah: but the men of the place were Benjamites.

And when he had lifted up his eyes, he saw a wayfaring man in the street of the city: and the old man said, Whither goest thou? and whence comest thou?

And he said unto him, We are passing from Bethlehem-Judah towards the side of Mount Ephraim; from thence am I: and I went to Bethlehem-Judah, but I am now going to the house of the Lord; and there is no man that receiveth me to house.

Yet there is both straw and provender for our asses; and there is bread and wine also for me, and for thy handmaid, and for the young man which is with thy servants: there is no want of any thing.

And the old man said, Peace be with thee; howsoever let all thy wants lie upon me; only lodge not in the street.

So he brought him into his house, and gave provender unto the asses: and they washed their feet, and did eat and drink.

Now as they were making their hearts merry, behold, the men of the city, certain sons of Belial, beset the house round about, and beat at the door, and spake to the master of the house, the old man, saying, Bring forth the man that came into thine house, that we may know him.

And the man, the master of the house, went out unto them, and sais unto them, Nay, my brethren, nay, I pray you, do not so wickedly; seeing that this man is come into mine house, do not this folly.

Behold, here is my daughter a maiden, and his concubine; them I will bring out now, and humble ye them, and do with them what seemeth good unto you: but unto this man do not so vile a thing.

But the men would not hearken to him: so the man took his concubine, and brought her forth unto them; and they knew her, and abused her all the night until the morning: and when the day began to spring they let her go.

Then came the woman in the dawning of the day, and fell down at the door of the man's house where her lord was, till it was light.

And her lord rose up in the morning, and opened the doors of the house, and went out to go his way: and, behold, the woman his concubine was fallen down at the door of the house, and her hands were upon the threshold.

And he said unto her, Up, and let us be going. But none answered. Then the man took her up upon an ass, and the man rose up, and gat him unto his place.

And when he was come into his house, he took a knife, and laid hold on his concubine, and divided her, together with her bones, into twelve pieces, and sent her into all the coasts of Israel . . .

Saul, on the eve of a battle, consults a necromancer, at Endor, so that she'll conjure up dead Samuel: 'And when the woman saw Samuel, she cried with a loud voice. [. . .] And the king said unto her, Be not afraid: for what sawest thou? And the woman said unto Saul, I saw [a god] ascending out of the earth. And he said unto her, What form is he of? And she said, An old man cometh up; and he is covered with a mantle.'

It's still a world close to the one that we discover in the glaring sunlight shining over the Golan Heights; up there, only stables and military barracks, many stones but also many flowers, most of them red or blue—reds and blues of an intensity that I think never to have seen elsewhere. An eagle is soaring above the watchtower overlooking the UN camp of Quneitra. Few visible traces of fighting; but, whether one wishes so or not, one thinks of it. Have the corpses been taken away, or are some of them buried there, with only rocks as steles—rocks like Jews place on their steles—and beneath the insolence of flowers?

I look at Mount Hermon covered with snow on the horizon and think of Lebanon extending from its base on the other side of the mountain, Lebanon whose name means whiteness and which almost has the same name as the moon, to which the Shulamite woman is compared in the Solomon's Song: 'Who is she that looketh forth as the morning [the dawn], / fair as the [white] moon'; she who, moreover, comes from Lebanon.

This is also immemorial. The snow still shines today on the rusted carcasses of tanks.

∂

At this point, a parenthesis needs to be opened, with the risk of never being able to be closed. It's because I'm touching upon, in these slight notes, infinitely complex problems that I cannot resolve, lacking the knowledge, the intelligence and the mental depth to do so; these notes, to a great extent, are unworthy of what they rub shoulders with; and obviously not being up to the task, I should feel uncomfortable enough not to publish any of them. Yet I've almost reached the end of the page, the end of the book that I'll have attempted to write—without whatsoever having wanted it to be like this; to the very last measures of this song that isn't exactly one. Shouldn't one have the courage and the energy to act consequently, while keeping in mind the imminence of the last word?

Obviously, these kinds of speech which, so I believe, I'm reading in landscapes and places as well as in architectures, amount to little; all this only grazes me; and the laziness, cowardliness and doubting spirit probably linked to them make me content myself with these light brushstrokes—as I've perhaps always done, in all fields.

Always, not even split or simply torn, but divided among various drives, accommodating myself too easily like all tepid people (but in all likelihood one is born tepid, and one cannot become fervent or imitate intransigence; and from this weakness that is given to you, as part of your makeup, like a physical weakness, you have to manage, and try to draw something good out of it. To do one's best with what one has and what one is could be the first great rule of conduct).

I saw, noticed, glimpsed this or that. I read, or thought to have read, signs that had appeared in front of me in an immediate way, sometimes stealthily, in and through my ignorance. If I've transcribed them, it's because they, at least for a moment, sometimes longer, *lifted* me higher than myself, or, rather, carried me to the best of what I could be. It was like so many peaks whose snow the evening light sets on fire or heats to the incandescence of snow.

However slight this can appear to be, I mustn't forget it, leave it unstated. All the philosophy of the world will not distract me from it—although the violence of the world can destroy it. I raised my eyes, for example, towards those apparently useless porticos: those who imagined and built them showed that they obviously possessed a light-hearted way of singing; they composed an aerial music in an open space. Elsewhere, they made graves look like fountains; people would sit on steps encircling the base of them. It can thus be imagined that people grew peaceful for a few moments. In this city full of weapons, I remember the place where there was air and, one storey below, shadow. One should be able to bend over the rim of the tomb of saints as over a well. I then experienced more or less the same feeling, as if I'd opened once again Rumi's *Divan* and, among many lines remaining mute for me, I'd come across these, for example:

> Death breaks the cage, but doesn't kill the
>   bird.
> How can death matter to the feathers of the
>   eternal bird?
> Remain silent. Long you have spoken and
>   no one heard
> from what terrace came the sound of this
>   drum and these words.

I wonder today if, even as I'd imagined a staging of scenes from Tasso's play in Muristan, the marvel wouldn't have been, that morning, to see whirling dervishes on the sunlit esplanade; although I've never been able to dance, I'd have better understood their trance more than the frenzied stamping feet of devout Jews, a little further down, their faces against the Wall.

In Israel, the signs of violence were everywhere; the never-ending signs of poverty and injustice, and the pungent hatred that ensues from them; everything that awakens the beast in us, that would awaken it in me as well, almost certainly, if I were one of those people, in their misfortune. If we're ever more on the brink of nausea today, it's not because of death per se, nor the imminence of one's own death: we were forewarned; it's contagion of evil. Has it worsened over time? This isn't even certain. What is certain is that we make up the first generations who can ignore none of its manifestations over the surface of the earth, that our minds are wounded daily by its images, by its noise; whereas our minds have never been—this is also certain—more disarmed, less firm, less hardy.

(Almost by chance, or, rather, to prolong my rereading of Hugo, I've recently discovered d'Aubigné: the perfect example of a kind of man who is completely different from us in a century that has nothing to envy of ours for harshness. His epic poem *Les Tragiques* already denounces the proliferation of evil; all the capital sins are fustigated therein, with almost the same force as in *The Inferno*; and like Dante who was involved in his century, d'Aubigné bore arms, fought and received blows. The worst was unable to disconcert him, to baffle him, because he believed that he possessed the truth, praised the Huguenot martyrs who had died to remain faithful to their religion and awaited, without a shadow of a doubt, the Day of Judgement, which already dazzles him with its promise: 'The air is now but sunrays, so sown it is with Angels'. Yet this man, like most of his contemporaries, had been wholly plunged into the most concrete, brutal reality; he knew what filth and stench are, and blood when it stops irrigating a body, stops lending to a body its most tender crimson colour and flows out of it, staining the dust and reddening the clearest water. What is extraordinary is that the God in whom he believes is apparently, to his eyes, as real, as indubitable as—and, in the final reckoning, infinitely realer than—all the most exquisitely or atrociously visible things of this world. Because of this, mustn't he also be seen as a precursor of today's fanatics, of all those for whom a Book that is proclaimed holy keeps indelibly engraved in its pages a Truth as evident and rigid as an iron prison bar or a bludgeon?)

Here I am, once again, with a foot in both camps, a ghost lacking a body, floating from one impulse to another, occasionally nostalgic for that unique Truth whose fruits have so often been admirable—even when I also see its share of errors, blindness, even lies, and am frightened by the crimes and massacres that it has induced. However, am I not going to be led to think that we'll have known authoritarian 'Truths' that have produced, more or less, only crimes and little goodness (the dictatorships of our century), and other religious 'Truths' which, although they've also been criminal, have built the most beautiful monuments on earth, raised souls to the highest part of themselves, given support to suffering hearts, and tried, in the cases of some religions, to master the beast inside us? Because these 'Truths' drew their energy from a hidden source which cannot be located on our maps, and is ever stealing away from us; or, to use another metaphor, lit by light coming from a hearth that remains ever out of reach? Perhaps, then, I could say this, almost in the final reckoning—and it is absolutely no longer an issue concerning just this trip to Israel in March 1993: that I have been touched, retained, delighted, fortified on such-and-such an occasion, even exalted, every time, whenever and wherever it has happened, that I had the impression of drinking water that had surged forth, after more or less long detours, from that secret source, or of seeing things being lit, even feebly, by light coming from a hearth that can never be located. One can imagine that this water and this light have been distributed from the beginning of our history in very diverse forms which they had to take on in order for us to be sensitive to them; as if they'd been incessantly translated and retranslated by unequally faithful and gifted translators. In this, at least, I'll have believed all my life long, simply because it seemed to me that this kind of emotion, which had all the appearances of spontaneity, of an immediateness anterior to all knowledge, could not 'lie'—which is still a belief and, as such, questionable, and perhaps a pure illusion. In the long run, nothing has appeared to me to be worth the trouble of writing down except this: no longer through the effects of a faith that would raise mountains and make you accept martyrdom to assert it, but borne up, all the same, by something like 'honesty', the need to give an account 'honestly' of the little that one has experienced that is essential, say, fertile—this term of 'honesty' thus supposing that one thinks that one can more or less near, all the same, a 'truth' . . . I'm obviously going round in circles, but can one do anything else in this circle that is your life and your limits? At the same time as your footsteps head straight for the wall, and that this barely glimpsed country still cannot manage to untie its knots of hate.

. . . What is more beautiful than the foliation of light-coloured leafs coming out on the oaks in the scree, on brittle branches covered with silver lichen? But isn't this the imagery of an old outmoded poet with his final budding of words? May they thus blossom fast on these mountain slopes! (One recent evening, while listening to some music, I had the idea of a line passing, flying above everything, fast like an arrow, or like the white bird back then over Citis pond, near Saint-Blaise; a line above everything, but I then thought, because I'd been working on these notes: 'above the Jordan River', which, at first glance, was not very meaningful; an extremely fast but firm line, like an arrow, like a paraph that would have vouched, but at the top of a page, for something written on the page; imperious and fleeting like the lightning bolt of a certitude.)

This was supposed to establish, who knows how, a link between thinking of the ephemeral and thinking of the eternal. Like, indeed, that foliation when there was only rarely a bird chirping, in fact more fearfully than joyously, to respond to it.

Someone could think this: soon, in a more or less brief lapse of time, you're going to lose everything, slowly or all of a sudden (all of a sudden would be better, but you cannot master this), every one of your senses, and the possibility to complain about it, if not to be frightened by it; and you'll perceive only ever-more rarely, and ever further and further away, hands and voices that will do their best to help you, as well as ever-more scattered and frail fragments of this world. The cause is understood, however vast is the pain that must be crossed, without those last footsteps leading to something else than the definitive impossibility of walking.

. . . So the time would have come to make an effort, to face up to this. Unless, on the contrary, one should let oneself become undone in the most natural way possible . . . And not pretend to be a soldier of any army. One isn't going to solve, *in extremis*, when not all of one's resources are even there any more, the enigma that has never been solved by anyone! One isn't going to be enlightened all of a sudden, when one is weak and hazy to that extent! (I've kept in front of my eyes for some time now, and I sometimes glance at it when I lift my eyes from my writing, a postcard featuring Rembrandt's *Pilgrims at Emmaus* at the Jacquemart-André Museum: there's no chance of having the face of that poor old man dazzled by He whom we see here only as a great shadow!) One expects no kind of enlightenment but, rather, the progressive distancing, the growing absence that I've observed in many old people, or a fathomless stupor and sadness, a humiliation, an infinite tiredness at having 'attained' this state; like most of them, one will be without bravery, without serenity; vanquished, quite simply, without glory; probably inferior to many in endurance, in dignity. I hold that for almost granted. So one might as well carry on regardless, as much as one can.

. . . They're dressed in black; they pervert the light of which they claim to be the servants. They like to hate, they delight in killing. Are there remedies for this? Ever since the Enlightenment, many people have said and still say: Education, Reason. But hadn't those who invented extermination and put it into practice in the camps been to school, hadn't most of them received in addition a religious education, a Christian one? As for the others in the East, didn't they—who, in accordance with Lucretius' vows, had gotten rid once and for all of the 'fear of gods', of the embarrassment of having to deal with gods, those who would at last take care of mankind 'here and now' without waiting any more for the so-called rewards of the Beyond, and heal all the evils—also continue to go delirious as well, in another way, and ultimately at the expense of mankind? And has anything been resolved by those who have, more recently—casting off all ideologies

and all rules because all rules and ideologies are per-
verted, limitative and arbitrary—nourished young
people with the illusion of happiness in anarchy, in
a perpetual party amid a general dissoluteness? It
seems, instead, that their marvellous yet extravagant
promises have left behind, everywhere, only groups
of suffering souls, emptied of that blood that would
otherwise have burst out in blossoms of fire, enfeebled
or shaken by sterile nervous shocks. It also seems
that the last subsistent source of energy is hatred: the
black and the red entangled on the walls of ruins in
Palestine.

. . . Nonetheless, one could imagine as travelling, from
one end of the world to the other, nameless groups
without flags, not sects whatsoever—which are all probably crews born out of cretinism—voyagers—in the
strict sense of the term or merely 'of the inner world—
more or less obscure, even sometimes shabby—nor
would they be superstars of wandering—; just people,
as they are, without explicit links among themselves,
but who would share an ability to persevere amid the
worst debacles, with the involuntary, not even heroic,
hardly conscious resistance of those insects, such as
scorpions, whose armour, it is claimed, would resist the
worst irradiation, whereas these people wouldn't even
wear armour or wouldn't want any; only the capacity,
sometimes, to have a frank or shy smile, a few movements of real compassion, now and then a gesture of

real goodness, an almost tireless patience; so it would seem that they'd received from life, after all, without having searched or asked for it, or without searching and asking for anything, or not much, light provisions for the journey, not the same provisions for everyone, but enough, until the opposite is proven, to keep them moving until their last breath—after which, silence! This would be a kind of last hope to hope for, that their footsteps—over paths outside and inside— tracing out, independently of belonging to any group or programme, freely, a network which, one wishes, would be as invisible and fertile as that formed by roots in the ground. We have friends among them; all our true friends, actually, are of this kind. We draw no vanity from this, we hardly speak about it, we neither enrol nor excommunicate anyone, we don't believe that we're authorized to teach anyone a lesson; but the awareness, or the dream, of this network is our less fragile support.

We walk as long as we can, gathering now and then those things whose quick fragrance modifies our relationship with the world and seem to dissolve its limits. It would be unfortunate not to give a little credit to this barely perceptible activity which has persevered since the dawn of time.

1993–1997

Post-scriptum

Seven years have gone by since I finished this uncertain text. The 'knot of darkness', the 'knot of hatred'— hasn't it tightened? Is there anything left of the mea-gre hopes that followed upon the so-called Geneva initiative? (For once, I'd been proud that my native country, too often too neutral, had supported it.)

It's strange that this long conflict, whereas I have no truly personal bonds with anyone on one side or the other, has weighed down to this extent on my mind during all these recent years. Is it perhaps because it exemplifies the painful, ferocious absurdity of so many other wars?

I suffer for a humiliated people. The voice of their great poet, Mahmoud Darwish, deeply touches me. Then when extremists, at the end of a Parisian march for Palestine, unfurl a banner soiled by the ignoble words 'Death to the Jews', I collide once again with the inextricable.

Should one have shouted, all one's life long, louder than henchmen and victims? But who, today, can 'shout in a just way', as the Prophets were supposed to have done, thereby overthrowing impious kings? The purest words end up as slogans on T-shirts or embroidered on silk scarves. I'm afraid that the power of money, proliferating like a plague, rots everything that is human down to the roots. (These are apprehensions, more than thoughts, but what thoughts will henceforth help?)

August 2004

A Calm Fire

To Marie and Gérard Khoury

A number of reasons, the best of which are only too painfully evident, have made me hesitate to publish these pages. What nourishes my scruples more than anything else is that the threat already weighing down on Lebanon when we went to the country on the pretext of giving two poetry readings, in 2004, has, far from vanishing, worsened since then to the extent that one no longer knows where to find anything that could kindle the slightest hope in us; and my case can only be aggravated by my choice, for these pages, of a title borrowed from a poet who couldn't help but ignore everything about the history of these places as it would take shape and subsequently become more complicated well beyond, or well short of, his inspired reveries.

All the same, something has obviously allowed me, rightly or wrongly, to surmount such legitimate scruples: this is because what I clumsily speak of here also belongs, after all, to reality; that all kinds of forms of beauty persevere, that friendship continues to exist in thousands of ways, as do hospitality, generosity and graciousness; even as occur moments of deep calmness, genuine exchanges and clear skies as indubitable as the blackest or stormiest clouds; so that persisting in gathering these signs and making a short, indeed modest book out of them is less an insult to the ordeals of these countries than a tribute paid to them and, in the final reckoning, doesn't add to the despair towards which almost everything leads us today.

With this same concern, and despite my ignorance in this field, I'm pleased to be able to let some snatches of the art of a few great poets from there be heard in these pages.

March 2007

. . . and quicker than I had thought
A Spirit then swept me away, far from home,
To where I'd never dreamt of going.
And in the twilight of dawn the shadows
Of the forest grew
As we flew
Over yearning streams
Of my homeland, then countries never known.
But soon, fresh and bright,
Secretive and through a golden haze,
Vaster with each step of the sun,
And fragrant with a thousand mountain peaks,
You opened up to me like a flower—

Asia!
And with dazzled eyes I sought
something familiar, for the wide streets
Were new to me, as from where
Gold-adorned Pactolus comes down from Tmolus,
Where Tauros and Messogis stand,
And where the garden, full of flowers,
Is aflame
With a calm fire! . . .

Hölderlin

THE THOUSAND AND ONE NIGHTS (1)

As circumstances had it, we'll have seen of Beirut, besides our friends' house which is now but an empty space, a phantom painfully laden with memories for them, as well as this or that ruined, scarred mansion preserved in memory of an especially atrocious war— but what war isn't?—only quarters that could still appear the best kept-up back then and mansions where affluence reigned—very far away, it must be said, from the camps of the Bedouins and the Palestinians glimpsed alongside roads where opulent orchards give way to arid fields bristling with black plastic debris or to muddy beaches.

From these contacts with a world which, in many respects, was still privileged, we'll certainly not forget an evening in the home of Ghassan Tueni, the head of one of the most important newspapers in Lebanon, a deputy from Beirut and an eminent diplomat, of whom I knew only about his political importance— and that his first wife, a talented poet who had died young, had inspired a 'stele', by Georges Schehadé, which happened to be one of my favourite poems in an *oeuvre* that had long been especially dear to my heart:

> She has left her friends' hand
> For a walled-in garden wholly blue
> Where the bird flies off with its nest

> Black eyes black hair
> And now all the beauties of shadow
> On her shoulders

More than twenty years had gone by since Nadia T.'s death. It would be Ghassan Tueni's 'new wife' who welcomed us, infinitely gracious herself as well (and how elegance can be a precious ornament of life when a smile without falsehoods accompanies it!), at the top of a grand staircase leading down to reception rooms where many people had already gathered, a situation that never makes me feel at ease. (But the presence of Dominique Fernandez, because we knew him a little and I like his zest for life and beauty, probably helped us to take off our coats of awkwardness— which had nothing sumptuous or oriental about them.)

I've neither the taste nor the talent for telling stories, so I'll not describe that evening, contenting myself with evoking a very beautiful mansion whose balcony looked out on tall trees and on the night; with conveying the mood of light-hearted cordiality that was circulating, among the guests, over exquisite food; and especially a warmth, I believe I can put it this way, a colourful warmth that enveloped us and that probably emanated from all these elements in a setting which, however, I really didn't notice much because it mattered little, provided that we let ourselves be borne along by it—even as, one day long in the past but unforgotten, we were impregnated with the fragrance of orange trees in the streets of Seville or Cordova.

The dishes that embellished the buffet tables were not piled with those pyramids of multi-coloured gems which Aladdin's mother, taking them for transparent pieces of fruit, offers to the Sultan—as depicted on an illustration in my old edition of a selection of *The Thousand and One Nights*, received as a gift by my sister in 1928, an edition which I must have stolen from her, since I still have it at hand, and whose sumptuous images have accompanied me all my life to nourish my reveries.

The storytelling was vague, but this mattered little: there was marvellousness back then even as there was here, a scintillation of jewellery, a flavour of rare spices; and the incense that the dervishes enveloped themselves in to have, for example, a door opened for them in the boulders, in the same book, must also, in another way, have been present in those rooms.

(May our hosts that evening forgive me: another image came back to me when we returned home: Delacroix's *The Women of Alger*, which, as everyone knows, does not specifically evoke a high-society evening; but this was only because of the particular kind of shadowy warmth that had reigned there from the onset and made it so easy, even for those who are awkward, even boorish like us in society, to be there, to speak, to eat, and to drink without the slightest restraint. A warmth similar to that flowing in the blood of some of Baudelaire's most beautiful verses and that is as deep and as vivid only there, in those twilights that he loved so, in those soft glowing fires, those reddish hues of hair; something, finally, that the single word 'Orient' still suggests in us—as opposed to a desert of warriors and ascetics.)

After dinner, our host led me in a most friendly fashion to see a few precious icons in what must have been his study. I was not surprised to learn that his big house was now called 'The House of the Poet', in tribute, of course, to Nadia Tueni's *oeuvre*, but also, more generally, to the idea of poetry—without any of the slight ridiculousness that is attached to the idea today when it is excessively toned down or, on the contrary, exalted without discernment.

When we left late in a still-mild October night, I realized that there were guards and dogs, at the entrance, to watch over the house, which usefully reminded me that *The Thousand and One Nights* were also filled with violence and cruelty. A few months later, alas, the nightmare would seem ready to begin again for the Lebanese, who had, moreover, never ceased fearing its return.

Worse: on 12 December last year—2005—as I was trying to give shape to this piece of travel writing, our host's son, Gebran Tueni, upon returning from Paris, was assassinated not far from his home.

My nationality has enabled me to be directly involved in no war. But when I think back on the past, I remember and still remotely hear the bells tolling the alarm in August 1939, throughout the mountain valley where we were on holiday for once, and announcing the general mobilization of the Swiss Army; and, after all, only a little would have sufficed for my father, who once again had put on his old captain's uniform, to be led, like others, into the calamity. I also recall, a few years later, those martyred hostages of Vercors, whose spectres made me write an awkward, yet sincere, *Requiem*. Ever since then, when will those very black clouds not have hovered over our lives and more or less near them, even when the real sky was clear to the extent of offering the hope—the illusion?—of a victorious light?

As so often during this trip, the next morning we'd be almost alone amid the ruins of Tyre as we followed the long column-lined walk that goes across the necropolis with its beautiful sarcophaguses sometimes dethroned and lying on their sides, knocked over like boats after a storm; and the enormous hippodrome apparently able to seat twenty thousand spectators was no more than an intensely luminous void. Such are the kinds of places where, as in front of all great ancient ruins, the great melancholy dreamers, following Chateaubriand's example, would have meditated on the more or less slow foundering of empires . . . But that day, far from the reigning silence that one wishes to find at great vestiges in order to try to hear the mute footsteps of Time, the air was shattered by the preaching, broadcast every now and then so that no one, anywhere, could escape it, of an imam raging against all the enemies, real or supposed, of Islam. We were not very far from the Israeli border, in a region of beautiful orchards, completely unhealed wounds and latent threats.

In space full and empty like a ring
Night's iron-railing gates are opening onto the sea
     or dreams
Tonight Mesopotamia and its windows are there
     on the plain
The rose is warming itself by the lamp like a sister
Oh look
A sailboat with a lion's head is anchoring
And ever on the beach
The big white wrinkles of the sea

Georges Schehadé

A MORNING IN BAALBEK

Baalbek will have been our first visit to a famous site, after we'd crossed the vast plain of the Bekaa Valley ... but I'll not waste my time redoing the *Blue Guide*, even if I were to embellish it. One year later, I only remember—and having taken next to no on-the-spot notes, because my mind wasn't active enough, my eyes not open enough, my heart not as sensitive as in the past—that after having raised my eyes towards the top of the portico with, perhaps, almost the same feeling of surprise and reverence that contemporaries must have felt (and only today, not at the time, have I recalled the Propylaea in Athens where, the uphill climb being slower towards more luminous ruins, I really imagined that I was climbing to the level of the gods), I knew that here was the presence of Rome, though with more colossal proportions, as I'd seen before only in Egypt with more than once, in fact, some despondency; this was Rome, that is—beginning with the entrance, there was no doubt about it—power that needed to be firmly established and glorified, along with the will to impose respect, if not fright, before a master more terrestrial than celestial, or both at the same time. The entire group of monuments was no less admirable for this, but perhaps more remote from us than the Acropolis . . . and thus, with these too long parenthetical remarks now finished: 'I only remember' that we long strolled within the immense space in which the ruins were enclosed, once again as almost the only visitors—which greatly changes how one observes—with a sort of, as I think I can say, happiness beyond all thinking: because we were four friends who got along harmoniously and were on a trip, because the weather was beautiful, the wars momentarily forgotten, as well as all the other shadows; because, less banally, there must have been in us, all the same, a mute pride at the thought that mankind had once been able to raise such monuments and that they'd lasted, even as ruins, still imposing their great proportions on the natural setting, drawing a calm, sovereign music from the stones and from nothing but the stones, a *Te Deum* or a *Gloria in excelsis Imperatori*; and even as in those kinds of music, between loud bursts of trumpets or cymbals, a melody can slip in that welcomes, and calls for, the grace of ornaments, I think that, in Baalbek as well, what most won me over was this or that finely crafted niche in the Hexagonal Court, this or that bas-relief decorating the low walls of the great basins of the Court of the Altar: 'nereids, fauns, sirens, tritons, medusas, garlands' (I'm quoting the *Blue Guide*): that is, all the feminine, vegetal grace needed by a basin, a fountain or a source to awaken, in the granite at the same time as in us, frail marvels as lasting as mountains. And I haven't forgotten my happiness at watching wild grass waving and at real flowers blossoming between the collapsed columns.

Columns: the 'Cantique' that Valéry devoted to them naturally came back to my mind when I believed, in turn, that I was hearing their music in the luminous air of that morning:

> Sweet columns, with hats
> trimmed with daylight
> . . . .
> Sweet columns, oh
> The orchestra of spindles . . .

But can one really write that columns are sweet and, even worse, rig them out with hats? Or did Valéry perhaps only have in sight the tiny columns and balusters of a boudoir? ('Disciple of spun glass', as Ponge once called him, as opposed to the 'crystal' of his mentor, Mallarmé . . .)

These columns aren't trees either, even if they were initially the transfiguration of them. But we almost never see them, and here not any more than elsewhere, as they once were: when they supported roofs. They calmly and powerfully give rhythm to space; they assert themselves, in regard to space, without enclosing it; and as the civilizations using them for the glory of their gods or their emperors become more refined, the columns carry high—here higher than everywhere else, so high that we can barely make it out—a kind of inflorescence, yet which remains stone-like, in defiance to the more or less fragile plants that could have served as models to the sculptors. Where only a few columns subsist in a line, raised even higher by their enormous pedestals—ah! One by no means imagines that they look like young women, even processioning towards some altar or some god!

Do the columns perhaps resemble nothing and is it thus futile to look for something equivalent? Nonetheless, this search isn't undertaken to embellish a piece of writing but, rather, in an attempt to translate simply the rapport which, today, can exist between those columns and a traveller who is as remote as we are from the world in which they were erected and who admires them all the same, which means that they speak to him, like a very high engraved inscription above those that he struggles to decipher, having lost so much of his Latin.

Ultimately, I believe that what I vaguely felt in front of those columns much resembled the impression of which I spoke one day in regard to a line of tall poplars: that they were like a filter for the air; apart from the fact that at Baalbek there was no quivering, no rustling, and that the proportions were considerably greater: so what was it, then? Rather than a filter, which is still too vague an analogy, did the columns form a sort of enormous stone harp, an instrument with intervals of air, or of light . . . that makes the memorable glory of all the kinds of kings resound up there?

(All the same: after quoting Valéry, one mustn't forget Charles Corm, one of whose poems is entirely reprinted in a small guide to Baalbek and ends like this:

> . . . Elsewhere the earth abounds
> With green grass and lawns,
> While here columns sprout
> From our seasons.
>
> Columns that stir,
> Until they swoon,
> The most insensitive zones
> Of the flesh of the horizons;
>
> Horizons that resound
> To the pleasures of liaisons
> Of porphyry and ozone
> Conjugated by reason.

To speak in verse myself:

> Who won out here
> Between rhyme and reason?

When we came out of the immense enclosure, it was hot—it was 26th October. A gardener was watering the oleanders of the small garden at the entrance; it seemed as though the strong hoarse voice of a muezzin was singing beneath the arches of water drops, giving rhythm to a beautiful day and appearing, this time, to be calling only for prayer and not for any crusade.

Here I am covered with the salt of my sins
O Good Sun deign to absolve and enlighten me
Have I not left the mobility of my eyes
On the sea to please you O Lord
And drowned all my brilliant faculties
Except for a rosary of tears in my hand
Except for a bit of stamina in my knees
And the desire to walk all the way to the snow

Fouad Gabriel Naffah

BUCKET WATERWHEELS 'LIKE STARS'

So here is Hama. We're apparently the only customers, or nearly so, in the immense Apamee Cham
Palace where, as we are leaving the next morning, the
receptionist, learning what my 'job' is, will go off to
find a few pages of her own poetry, in French, and
offer them to me—a friendly gesture to which I'll
respond by offering her my poems translated into
Arabic. It's true that in this late season and under
the circumstances of the time, she must have enough
time to read and to write. And in the big windowed
restaurant where we'll have dinner, there's hardly
anyone besides local customers, of whom a few young
women who are nothing less than veiled, smoking the
hookah and listening with only a distracted ear to the
musicians supposed to be enlivening this too-vast
dining room in which, in addition, it's cold, as if the
water rising in sprays from the big norias beyond the
windows were already splattering us. Those big
wooden bucket waterwheels, the first of which were
built in the Middle Ages to solve the irrigation problems of the neighbouring countryside situated at a
higher elevation than the Orontes River, have today

inevitably become a tourist attraction, so much so that one approaches them suspiciously. But they've always astonished people and been a topic of conversation. As early as the twelfth century, Ibn Jubayr, returning from a pilgrimage to Mecca, writes: 'It's an ancient, famous city. It hasn't spread out very far, nor does it have beautiful buildings. It's hemmed in and its houses are heaped up on each other. It's not pleasurable to look at, since it seemingly veils its charms. But a secret beauty can be discovered by exploring the town and walking through its neighbourhoods. To the east flows a big river that widens when it's joined by its tributaries. On both banks, bucket waterwheels face each other and from there gardens extend continuously, the branches of whose trees dangle over the water, their foliage like down on cheeks. The river winds between shady areas and flows with the same harmony'. Two centuries later, Ibn Battuta evokes in turn this 'marvellous city' [. . .] surrounded by gardens and orchards where bucket waterwheels turn like stars'.

It's night as we approach this area through narrow, dimly lit streets between old houses with nearly windowless walls. In front of the entrance to a hammam that is still open, a few men are quietly sitting or squatting on stone benches, smoking or not smoking, speaking slowly, softly. A passer-by accompanied by his young son exchange a few words in Arabic with our guide and friend. But as we move on, the noise of the waterwheels increases, a music of creaking and cracking in marvellous harmony with what we're beginning to see above the walls, those enormous wheels from which water, scintillating in the shadows, is streaming down—and where we also notice the workshop of a carpenter hard at work. The water-wheel is like an enormous machine, with slow wooden gears, seemingly imagined by Piranesi. A combination of a slow powerful movement, like the wheels of a cart for giants struggling up a slope, a din as powerful and seemingly laborious, and, finally, another noise, that of water, the scintillation and coolness of water lifted in this way up to the aqueduct—all this was, after the quiet narrow streets and in the darkness of night, something monumental, very old and very venerable which, for a few moments, made us contemporaries of the most remote fables. It was thereby all the stranger for us, as we came out of the maze of narrow streets, to be caught up by completely different rhythms and a completely different kind of noise, those of cars blindly speeding down the large avenues of a modern district, and that crowd of pedestrians who were all heading towards streets with violently lit shops where it was clear that more videos were sold than Qurans. And there, for the first time—but this would often be the case in other big cities—one couldn't help but wonder, with uneasiness, how the old and the new world would adapt to each other: that of veiled women wearing black gloves and of platinum blondes; of gloomy bearded men raging against the perverse Western World; of young people wearing jeans, hooked on slot machines; of the din of car-crammed streets and of the silence of the mosques when they give shelter only to those who are meditating.

Damascus
Caravan of stars on a green carpet
Two breasts of embers and oranges

Damascus
A loving body in his bed
like the bow
and the new moon
Open the bottle of time in the name of water

Revolve every day
in your nightly orbit
Fall in sacrifice
into the volcano you crave

The trees are sleeping around my bedroom
My face is apple and my love
island, pillow

And won't you come
Damascus
O bed
O fruit of night

Adonis

A STOPOVER IN DAMASCUS

In the twelfth century, Ibn Jubayr writes:

> Damascus, the paradise of the Orient, the spot from which its beaming light rises, the seal of the Islamic countries that we have visited, a new bride whom we admired after she'd removed her veil. Decked out with flowers and aromatic herbs, Damascus emerged wearing the green brocade gown of her gardens. She was eminently beautiful, adorned in all her finery as she sat on the bridal throne. Damascus takes pride in having given shelter to the Messiah and his mother— God bless them!—during their quiet stay on a hill covered with thick shadows and welling with streams whose water resembles that of Salsabil in Paradise . . .

(This allusion to the Messiah is based on a passage of the surah 'The Believers': 'We have made / the son of Mary and his mother into a Sign. / And we have given them refuge / on a quiet hill with streams'. But nothing says that Damascus is actually being described.)

As to Ibn Battuta, he quotes several poems glorifying Damascus, notably these lines:

> Lightning bolt, be the messenger of my tender greeting which will resemble your streaming water?
>
> Surprise Damascus at dawn with your slender arrows of rain and the flowers of the gardens will be inlaid and crowned with dew.
>
> Let the tails of your cloud pass over the quarter of Jayrun and, above all, choose an abode draped in nobility,
>
> Where the abundant spring lavishes its gifts and where the springtime shower has furnished the fodder.

Even if one takes into account that hyperbole didn't frighten the authors of these beautiful tributes, it goes without saying that reality comes up far short of this, today.

It's been a long time since people have ridden around Damascus on donkeys and camels. Here, like everywhere else, cars, buses, lorries and motorcycles have invaded. On broad avenues like 'Straight Street', which anarchic archaeological digs have currently made narrower, cars and pedestrians hurry along elbow to elbow, as it were, as they also do further on and closer to the souks: as in Cairo where it's ten times worse, there are surely too many people for too little room here. And although one feels no fear in these crowds, and although the pedestrians are unaggressive (ah, all the same, I saw a knife blade flashing during a rather lively argument between merchants in the souks!), one cannot help but think of what would happen in a crisis, whatever its cause; and of how quickly crowds, by the very fact of being crowds, can give in to panic.

Let's go beyond these thoughts, which have definitely become too trite, in order to retain a single, almost pious, image of Damascus: as we were leaving the hustle and bustle of the souks where we'd vainly sought to find, for a friend of ours, a beautiful kind of paper that had perhaps never been sold there among the overabundant cheap Qurans with their glossy bindings, the little square that opens out in front of the south side of the Great Mosque offered a kind of respite and made our heartbeats slow down with the same effects that music can have when we listen to it with all our being. Once we'd taken off our shoes and our wives had become unrecognizable false monks beneath green hooded frocks, the act of walking into the great courtyard of the Mosque with its shiny marble pavement surrounded by arched galleries and dominated by three minarets (including the 'Jesus' Minaret' from which the Messiah is supposed to come down on the Day of Judgement for the greatest pleasure of the Damascenes—cheerful fables that seem so sadly remote today), of strolling in this vast sunny quadrangle, and of seeking out the beautiful mosaics that recall those of Ravenna and Byzantium (as if one wanted us not to feel too strongly that we were strangers here—the trees and palaces of dreamy paradises hardly differ from one cultural world to another), was like the second movement of a progression readying us for our entryway to the great prayer room. Therein, a tender kind of shade was reigning and especially a sort of joyful tranquillity that I'd never experienced in a Christian church and that was probably enhanced by the presence of beautiful rugs seemingly inviting everyone to take a rest and be silent. At the base of a column, women were sitting and speaking among themselves without raising their voices but without whispering either; two of their children were clambering up a beautiful pink marble basin, as children are wont to do when playing, but not turbulently. Small glass-paned bookcases probably containing holy books were standing against a wall; a young religious man had removed one of them to look up something or read some prayers. Elsewhere, at the base of other columns, more elderly, bearded men were crouching while others were lying on the floor, dozing or slumbering. Among them, an old man who was wearing a white silken garment embroidered with gold facings must have been a dignitary of one of the numerous sects (if this is indeed the term) which divide Islam and between which, too often, it's torn apart. Both my heart and my eyes were full of astonishment, even marvel, as I was looking at all this, as if entering this place had made centuries vanish and allowed me to recover a world of which I'd dreamt when I was a child bent over images that I'd never forget; but I was also looking on with a kind of joy, and this joy was even more precious because it was linked to our world today: to its excesses, its lies, all its expressions of scorn, fear and hate, and its terrible acts of violence and savagery. Not that I'm neglecting these aspects because of a simple image and, indeed, a brief feeling of amazement: I'm not naive to that extent. All the same: we'd entered a place in which an extraordinarily natural peace was reigning—a peace which was as natural as the nearby din of the souks and in which neither constraint, nor reverential fear, nor exaltation, were blended. At that moment, the Great Mosque was no longer but a great motherly house, a place for halt and rest, or a caravanserai raised to a higher dignity: conversation, playing, meditation, prayer and sleeping beneath the eagle's wing that the cupola is supposed to represent; beneath Allah's wing.

It mattered to me that I'd seen this—not in order to forget the tyrants, the henchmen, the crusaders and the fanatics who unfortunately live and also act beneath these skies, for whatever sundry and unequally legitimate reasons have motivated them. And it mattered to me that I'd seen those children in their blue smocks coming out of school in a village lost in the middle of vast almond and pistachio orchards—children like. all children in countries where they're loved and respected; or that skinny old man who, once we'd asked him how to find some little-known church, had jumped onto his bicycle to lead us there and inform the guardian; or so many other simply human moments to contrast later, once we were back in the West, to all those hateful scenes the too-frequent vision of which, wilfully or not, distorts the way we think about the world.

And this, too, on another day, as we were walking along the wall of a mosque against which stood a very long stone or marble bench—and the same noisy, but unexcited crowd was still in the street down which we'd walked: eight or ten old men sitting side by side, leaning on their canes and draped in white. All of them were blind. The scene sufficed to bring me back once again to *The Thousand and One Nights* of my childhood . . . and to muse that those blind men had probably not lost their sight as had Baba-Abdalla for having been too greedy in front of the treasures that a dervish had been foolish enough to let him glimpse. But what difference was there between the old men and him, the hero of the tale, if it weren't that the dervishes had vanished or lost their power, and that the sultans of today show only rarely, or never, the noble clemency of Harun al-Rashid?

I'm still alive in your ocean. You didn't tell me
  what
a mother tells her sick son. I fell ill from the copper
moon on the Bedouin's tent. Do you remember
the road of your exile to Lebanon, where you forgot
  me
and the bag of bread? (It was wheat bread.)
I didn't scream so I wouldn't wake the guards. The
  scent of dew
set me on your shoulders. Oh gazelle who lost
there its shelter and its mate . . .

Mahmoud Darwish

PALMYRA

No more here than elsewhere do I wish to evoke ghosts of heroes, be they enchanting or prestigious. I saw only what I saw, as one who is nearly ignorant and forgetful of nearly everything, an old man who, having entered the cold season, rarely gets carried away about anything any more; but who nonetheless saw something about which it matters to him to say something. (A long time ago, maybe I'd have known how to say it in a single weightless poem, but I've lost the secret or the key—that no hand will ever tender to you again.)

Palmyra, palm grove: one could of course delude oneself with these words, all the more so in that, after all, they're appropriate. But 'Beware of Poetry!' False poetry lies in wait for you when a place is especially beautiful, and this one is much more so than others; and famous, and praised, and much visited—although less so today, as it's laden with anxiety.

How should I proceed? At the time, I took no notes. And the little that I've read will be of no help to me.

We left the hotel—which has the charm of patina and the good point of letting itself be forgotten once one has left it—as docile tourists whom the *Blue Guide* enjoins to get up early enough to see the sunrise on the nearby ruins and sands. At that end of an October night, the cold was biting, almost aggressive for anyone who had left his sleep grudgingly. I don't think anyone else was walking there; only a dog that was wandering around at random, nearer and realer than everything else, would soon join up with us; for indeed, in what was initially mere greyish weather, we had the impression of not being entirely awake and of finding ourselves in a limbo world where even the beautiful columns that we were approaching seemed made less of marble than haze. This makes me think, as I'm once again revising, for the umpteenth time, the translation rashly undertaken when I was sixteen or seventeen years old, of that 'Tenth Duino Elegy' where the young dead man is led by a Lament into a landscape that grows ever-more silent as he enters more deeply into it. (But at the time, I by no means thought of this.) Except that here, it would be the opposite: a world before birth, where a cold wind would still be blowing and where nearly no colours would yet exist; and would the stray dog perhaps help us, 'in reality', by being a friendly guide?

Then colours started emerging in which, while grey subsisted like a veil that would end up fraying, ochre was especially present, the most subtle hues of ochre, and a beginning of pink; the avenues traced by the narrow columns could be made out more precisely, became stone once again, yet as much in harmony with the sands as tree trunks are with the fields and meadows from which they seem to be born. They were, however, not trees (the place was entirely without foliage, completely without vegetation, as I realize only today while rediscovering it like a dream); those columns were not, as it would have been tempting to imagine them because of their elegance, a procession of young women—even if one could have recalled that Ulysses, facing Nausicaa, had found no more beautiful praise for her than to compare her to the trunk of a young palm tree; these were columns that had survived destruction and that were now beginning to turn pink, to bathe in the sun, while it was a little less chilly at their feet . . . And then, what was it?

What was it, there, facing us, around us, slowly taking shape beyond the limbo of dawn, in the sands, whereas we were soon no longer going to be completely alone and the first noises of cars were grating against the silence a little further off?

The truth is that, surely because I'm not enough of a historian, and as strange as it might seem during this walk before daybreak that we'd soon break off because even the first rays of sunlight couldn't keep us from continuing to shiver, I didn't think of tales of a glorious past, of power, of scheming, of passions, of all those tales without which, however, we wouldn't have been there, both captivated and shivering. I wasn't seeking to revive those vestiges of avenues, theatres and temples by imagining a 'motley' or 'raucous' crowd—as one wouldn't fail to say; even less so, as something 'picturesque': no 'peplum'! No. What was admirable there, I think, was the *measure* that still imposed itself, even fragmentarily, on the desert; that imposed itself, not to dominate it—or, all the same, indeed, initially to dominate it—but, as we would see all this today, to raise up that which is sterile, seemingly suitable only for erasing our footsteps, to an unforeseeable space unexpectedly blossoming in a way only human constructions can accomplish; and, ultimately, I wonder if what appeared there as it did often elsewhere were not as if we were reading, engraved on the increasingly clear sky, fragments of hymns similar to those called 'Homeric', invented to measure an already threatening world; to give it rhythm not with the goal of a conquest but in a movement of joyful procession in which something of the grandeur of the henceforth absent gods would have been instilled so that everyone would be reminded of a fertile agreement, translated or merely invented, between the earth and the sky.

I remember, today of course since I was too busy looking while we were there, Hölderlin's famous 'Song of Fate':

You walk up there in the light
  On soft ground, holy Spirits!
   Gleaming godly breezes
   Lightly graze you,
    As if a woman's fingers
     Were plucking holy strings.

The Heavenly Ones breathe
  Like a chastely guarded
  Sleeping infant,
   Like a modest bud,
   The Spirit eternally
   Blooming in them,
    And their holy eyes
    Gaze into the calm
    Eternal clarity.

But it is our fate
  To find no rest anywhere.
  Suffering, human beings
  Stumble, fall blindly
   From one hour to the next,
    Tossed off like water from cliff to cliff,
   Downward, for years,
   Into uncertainty.

So something of those daydreamt footsteps of the gods
was still preserved today in those colonnades and pure
arches, and it was no mirage: it was as if—slightly, of
course—we'd gone out only to discover the gods
coming back under cover of dawn.

And once the figure of Hölderlin had surged forth again in my mind, inevitably—for few of our Western poets will have been so magnetized by Asia, by that nearby Asia where Greece, which he loved above all, and then Rome, were also so present—I also remembered that in one of his poems, he who had known of the ancient world only a little of Provence (yet even this is uncertain, for his mind was already deranged), the name of Palmyra appeared, full of all the magic of which I could now verify the real power:

'Ages of Life'
You cities of the Eurphrates!
You streets of Palmyra!
You forests of columns in the desert plains,
What are you?
Your crowns,
As you crossed
The bounds of those breathing,
Vapour of smoke and the fire;
Now though I sit under clouds (each
Has its own calm) amidst
A pleasant stand of oaks on
The heath where deer gather, and strange
They appear, dead to me,
The spirits of the blest.

One of the most beautiful poems, but that transferred to these ruins, which the poet would never see, the thought of *hubris* and of its punishment by the gods, a thought familiar to him since he'd deeply meditated on the Greeks and had translated *Oedipus the King*. Whereas in that October dawn, in Palmyra, as well as at twilight on the same day, when I'd remain alone and quiet for a while, once again in the company of a stray dog, watching the night almost efface the ruins one after another, like music returning to silence—that of the harps lightly plucked by the woman musician's finger in 'Song of Fate'—while the compact block of the Arab citadel, a true boulder crowning the mountain, would stay pink and mauve longer, no thought of divine ire and simply even conflict would come to my mind. I could almost have said, would almost have taken the risk of saying this, if the place had vaguely inspired a remote similarity: that one day an orchestra as vast as a city must have gathered there, but that I'd reached this place too late to find anything but a vast enclosure, or a terrace, which was nearly deserted except for a few musical instruments that had been left behind, here and there, at random, perhaps because they were more difficult to transport than the others; and that their taut strings in those finely carved wooden bodies, or the skins of big drums that were barely out of tune, would have still vibrated for me even though all the musicians had long left.

Or else, it had been like a choir which, gathered together, would have produced an unbearable volume of sound; whereas since we'd arrived so late, to hear again a voice that was feeble yet pure, a voice here and a voice there rising without obeying any choirmaster, for itself, as the flame of a little fire warming these last singers would have done, a few persistent voices; and, better than a whole orchestra or a whole choir, this slight thing also joined up again with the 'holy Spirits' on high, beckoned to them without beckoning to them, bringing them back indeed because it was not beckoning to them, not bothering them, not imploring them.

('Beware! Danger of Poetry!' . . . I fear I've spotted the sign too late.)

At least a few words about the graves need to be said; either that they rise like towers—which, I believe, is relatively rare among funereal customs—or, in that they have been dug into sandy soil as in Egypt, one goes down into them by means of gently sloping ramps; and about the sculpture, peculiar to Palmyra and indeed rather monotonous, though less so than its Egyptian counterpart, and, all the same, quite beautiful.

The poses show dignity, the faces look reserved, very calm, rather inscrutable; the eyes look beyond you. It's again as if one were walking through a world of phantoms, but phantoms with a very noble shape and so pure that one would hesitate to disturb them by lingering too long. 'Guarded by silence and courtesy', as Saint-John Perse wrote of princely personages whose names I no longer recall; guarded as well by the ornaments adorning them, as if they could hope that headwear, diadems, jewellery and beautiful folds of cloth helped them to go over the last border and become integrated into a world that could only be the transfiguration, the fulfilment of a beauty merely sketched out in mortal life. Perhaps as well that the very matter in which these faces have been sculpted has something tender and warm to it, making them a little less remote, as if the wing of the evening, which had grazed them while they were alive, were accompanying them maternally, one last time.

And in these vaults some of which seem, all the same, a little too tidy, a little too bright once the heavy door has been opened for us—but it was not made to be used like that—how touching and precious then becomes the slightest trace of blue or green that takes us back to our sky and to our meadows of fragile living human beings!

Beauty of her toenails fruited with snow
On this side of the light where she's a statue
Strange and shiny and somewhat dead
Beneath the cold of the cold trees, of a tear
They've fallen asleep within the music, broken violins
Burning with that which was: strange leaves
Frozen on the other side of the fire

. . . And all these nests!
And all these bodies in the orange groves!
That feebly beat in the twilight
As in a disaster of the mind the violent heart
Aged beneath the moans of a turtledove
On this very poor side of love
In its fragrance of urine and jasmine

Salah Stétié

NOTHING BUT STONES, OR ALMOST

I must admit that, if I decided to take this trip to
Lebanon and Syria, two years after having somewhat
impolitely cancelled a first project, having failed to
muster the courage to go through with it, this was
because I'd seen, at the home of the friends who were
going to take us there this time, photographs of what
are called the 'dead cities' of the calcareous mountains
near Alep, and the ruins of Saint Simeon Stylites;
photographs which immediately reminded me of the
Armenian churches, discovered in 1998 in a beautiful
album on Armenian art, and which truly fascinated
me, inciting me to try to write a few short texts about
them. I don't think it's useless to add them here, as if
in the margins and as a prelude to this chapter:

'One is stopped short, grasped by something (while
looking, moreover, at simple photographs).

The thought crosses your mind that *no longer
anything*, in all of contemporary art, can stand up to
this (rightly or wrongly, probably wrongly, but it's
this thought that comes to you; it's likely less than a

thought, but neither has it come to you without any reason whatsoever).

One also says that, of the few trips that one would dream of running the risk to take, this would be the most tempting one.

Why this one?

One recalls one's jubilation when discovering Sant'Antimo in a wheat field, in Tuscany—and just as well, so many other churches in front of which one has lingered, without faith, or with so little faith, in life: Is the same thing at stake?

There's some of the same thing, and also something else.

What is the same is to have found in a few churches or a few temples one of those dwelling places where sacredness, like a distant heart, is still beating, still glimmering, like a very weak yet very steady flame.

The something else must be where these chapels, these churches, are located: in out-of-the-way places, in deserts and mountains, *on the borders*.

Like watchtowers or defensive towers, at outposts; built in places where the danger is greatest: "But where there's danger, / Also grows what can save," writes Hölderlin in "Patmos".

Buildings sometimes the colour of rust, or lava.

Raised stones, amid the scree.

Like someone who would be standing at the most exposed place.

(And a foliage motif, a thin arch, suffices for showing that it's only a casemate, a pylon, or a covered well.)

It's stone, raised among stones, and stone that was measured, mastered, made into a song.

Massive, compact churches, to better preserve their invisible core. Built to resemble the mountains looming over them, yet tamed by the mind.

Enclosures of their god in embryo.'

Venturesome notes to which I must add, hardly more in the margins, this complementary passage:

'Although I was not immediately aware of it, behind all this was the memory of *Journey to Armenia*, through which I discovered Mandelstam, in 1973, and his electrifying prose, his "horseman's" prose written by a man oppressed in every respect who had found in that country, all at once, vast expanses, the great outdoors, colours, "streams catastrophically rushing down the streets", and the sacred mountain of Ararat; a man who had really seen some of these churches; and he at least had been able to speak about them: "The first shock—a sensual shock: the very matter from which the old Armenian churches were made. / The eye searches for a form, an idea, expects it, but stumbles instead on the mouldy bread of nature or on a stony pie. / The teeth of your vision crumble and break when you look for the first time at Armenian churches"; and especially farther on: "The little church in Ashtarak is one of the most ordinary kind and, for Armenia, submissive. It is a little church in a six-sided headdress with a rope ornament along the cornices of the roof and the same sort of stringy eyebrows over the meagre mouths of its chinklike windows. / The door is quieter than water, lower than grass. I stood on tiptoe and glanced inside: but there was a cupola inside, a cupola! / A real one! Like the one in St Peter's in Rome, above the thronged thousands, the palms, the sea of candles, and the Pope's sedan chair. / There the recessed spheres of the apses sing like seashells. There we have the four bakers: north, west, south, and east, who, their eyes plucked out, knock into the funnel-shaped niches, rummage about the hearths and the spaced between the hearths and find no place for themselves. / Whose idea was it to imprison space behind this wretched cellar, this beggar's dungeon—in order to render it there a homage worthy of the psalmist?" '

After which I'd experience the deep shock of his poems, and indeed, among the most radiant ones in his *oeuvre*, the cycle titled *Armenia*, written while he was there during that autumn—blessed for him—of 1930 (whereas his slow descent into the inferno had already begun), in the jubilation of having set foot on this land of origins, in that clay in which he also read the first book of humanity: a land which had also often been oppressed, yet from which Mandelstam had drawn the food of his most solar challenge to every kind of destruction.

And this as well, the last note in the margins: 'it was André du Bouchet who had translated *Journey to Armenia* into French, with his son Gilles; and it was André du Bouchet and I who had dreamt of traveling together to the churches of the Realm of Ani; that neither he nor I will have seen.'

In compensation, there will have been, in the autumn of 2004, a whole day of wandering through 'calcareous mountains' in search of 'dead cities'.

What would first need to be shown is that this territory is but a great disorder of rocks, as if following a cataclysm, and that walking isn't always easy. However, it's not a desert, for there are olive trees and vineyards, expanses of rose-coloured ground, trails through wild plants and grasses. Rugged, hardly affable places, yet with a solid stratum. Places by no means funereal, yet severe, bare, of which one thinks, that in order to live there, it would be necessary to muster one's patience, to be frugal and tough. With all this, a chaos everywhere crowned with lots of air, armoured with light.

There's nothing surprising, then, about the fact that at Al-Bara, which has nearly vanished, and at Serjilla, which is more distinct and better preserved on its hillside, the little that remains of the graves, the churches and the houses can barely be distinguished from the landscape in which these small towns were established at the very beginning of the Byzantine era, between the fifth and seventh centuries, when the commerce of wine and olive oil was prosperous. What still stand and sometimes jostle against each other in front of our astonished eyes are walls truly like fortresses, walls built of big, heavy blocks of stone bonded together like pieces of ramparts rejecting any kind of welcome, to better protect, behind them, vulnerable lives and precious resources.

On the arid hillside of Serjilla, the stone is orange and grey, the colours of fire and ash, glints of some immemorial fire, colours that somewhat warm up the severe monumentality of its ruins. One has—at least the ignorant traveller who I was—much trouble imagining this place as a lively one in remote past centuries; moreover, no voice rose other than the harsh, hoarse one of the building stones, and on them there was almost no room for ornamentation, even of the most rudimentary kind: real flowers are less rare among the jostled stones than the sculpted flowers which would have attenuated the haughty rigidity of the forms. How they are humanized by the remains of a loggia with its three or four small columns that lighten and aerate the walls! For it's clear here, inasmuch as one wishes to imagine such an inhabited city, that it's initially men who will seem suitable to it, men holding heavy tools or weapons at the base of these iron- and rust-coloured walls; as if nothing of the gracefulness of women, of the turbulence of children, could leave traces for us in such a place.

A grandeur that astonishes, as if one were attending the first attempts at cajoling the boulders by metamorphosing them into dwelling places, by imposing an order on the disorder of the stones that is all the simpler in that it is more savage. And it will take a long time—actually not so much when measured against human history—for ornamentation to flourish beneath the sculptors' chisels, and soon become overabundant, under the eyes of less and less austere gods.

Qalb Loẓe: I remember the guardian who opened the rusted iron grille that gave access to the church; the children came running just as soon from the nearby village, joyously climbing up on the windows of the apse, boys and girls displaying little squares of cloth embroidered—by their mothers, by themselves at school?—which they wish to sell us and which one or another of us would surely have bought if the young woman guide accompanying us had not prevented us from doing so, concerned as she is to protect, from this still-hardly-aggressive form of begging, the tourists to come—on the influx of which some people count in her country to develop it and open it up more to the world.

Except for this, what can I—who have a very little bit of sense—say to give even a slight account of the admiration that I felt back then, on that morning of 5 November 2004, facing Qalb Loze? The memory is already a little blurred—it's entirely the fault of old age; and photographs, whatever they are, even the most beautiful ones, always remain so remote from the thing seen! So many more or less imponderable elements contribute to the emotion that overcomes you in such moments: intense light, of course, but also space—distances, perspectives; the more or less clear-cut, simultaneous perception of a few poor nearby houses, of the arid, very vast landscape beyond them; the presence of a few animals, a goat perhaps, a dog, some poultry, and of those children whom I mentioned who have no other relationship to these ruins than the hope of drawing some coins from the people who, still few in number, have come, sometimes from very far away, to see the ruins.

So in this great arid landscape with nothing but poverty in the environs, where one stares into the distance, through light that is almost harsh by dint of brightness and strong like the stones, this monument as an ordering of the stones scattered all around it, like the elevation of the simple idea of a house to the height of He the idea of Whom the house must at once shelter and celebrate; as if back then a presence of the Very High, in a thought woven of earth and air, had floated in the air, by means of an imperious necessity to bear this thought towards the highest conceivable objects, even as the Sun had naturally first been chosen for adoration; and now, it was an invisible sun, at once inner and inaccessible, to which grace and glory needed to be given by inventing a theology worthy of it, and an architecture that translated it in stone.

A few centuries later, all this would come alive, become more precise, and more intricate, until it attained a virtuosity in which, little by little, the freshness, the purity of this first encounter with the Very High would wear down and end up vanishing. Here, what impresses us—we who have been able to run our eyes over the entire trajectory from the birth to the death of this great art of churches—is to find ourselves once again at the beginning; for example, to see the earth and the sky through these very big arches that give measure and rhythm to them, that master them; and these first garlands or braids adorning them and also perfectly measured, as when, in music, above a basso continuo which is the 'ground', indeed 'obstinate' as one aptly termed it, a melody that is apparently freer and, in any case, more tender, rises in volutes.

A visible music, with its colours of earth, iron, sand and rust, to enclose, to hide 'something' which, being hidden, will shine forth even better outdoors.

Fortresses from which the only arrows shot out were the rays of that hidden sun, castles for pigeons today, if there are some, and back then for the purest Dove. This moment of architecture where the first leaves come out on the stones as they do on branches at the end of winter.

I wonder today if there weren't here, as already in Baalbek, without our necessarily being aware of it, in our emotion at Qalb Loze and, even more intensely a little later, at Qalaat Semaan, a sort of pride, all the same, that mankind had been able to accomplish this, when we so often tend to cultivate sentiments of shame because of the evil with which mankind has seemingly wished to illustrate itself for decades in a sort of frenzy—a meticulous frenzy, moreover, in some cases, which is the worst of all.

Thus, naturally, while discovering deep inside ourselves this emotion of pride, which is rare and also an emotion of joy, we're alarmed that it's almost always provoked by the past, more than by the present, where little can be found to nourish it except the marvels of science and technology, true marvels, indeed, but which lack that invisible element that has given rise to these sunbathed ruins at which we have

made a stopover, these past days, with a happiness—
despite everything—without melancholy; as if a heart,
a secret heart, were missing from the new marvels.

Of Qalaat Semaan, therefore, which is Saint Simeon
Stylites for us, I've nothing to add except that its music
is less coarse, less severe, more intricate, with more
deftness as well—those capitals that imitate leaves
bent over by the wind!—the most beautiful of all.

It's said that Simeon was the son of a peasant from
Sicily and born in 386; that at the age of sixteen he
entered a monastery on Mount Hermon and that, ten
years later, he joined the community of Deir Semaan;
where what could be called his 'records' of asceticism
drew such a crowd of pilgrims that he resolved to
escape them by settling on the top of a column which,
first only 3 metres high, would subsequently be raised
to 20. A column from which he's said to have exhorted
the pilgrims, advised visitors and even the Emperor
of Byzantium. He apparently didn't leave his shelter
until his death in 459.

Whatever share one gives to the inevitable exag-
gerations of hagiographists, this kind of madness
undoubtedly remains—it was, moreover, not unique
at the time; and how can one not still be astonished
today, especially today, that it was around this still-
standing pistil, which bears witness to this unwavering
passion, that the admirable stone rose of the church

bloomed. At least one can think that hate was not preached there.

Today, the mystical madness seemingly knows only how to destroy; or build what is false. This obviously inspires questions that are beyond my limits: Is it that the sense of the sacred was 'true', or should one say 'whole', 'full', flawless, in such a place and such a time, 'full' enough to give rise to an equally true and full expression, and notably in the stone of the temples and the churches? And, in addition, is this expression perfectly in harmony with the place where it took shape? And does this expression, or translation, appear less and less admirable and touching to us as faith weakens, changes, to the extent that the architecture ends up enveloping only emptiness?

The rest of us, Eliot's 'hollow men', would thus be all the more astonished, impressed and moved by the ruins and remains of 'sacred' eras because we can almost no longer imagine this plenitude and because we're ourselves empty in a world of juxtaposed kinds of emptiness where it sometimes seems that we can no longer do anything but let ourselves sink.

Except that we sometimes still experience shock in front of monuments with a vanished plenitude; except that we're still not indifferent when we go by them—on the contrary, since they have sometimes appeared to us more 'beautiful' than anything else, like beings of a completely distinct species—but I also fear that those beings already no longer exist and that we could not even speak to them; and all the while, we're sure that no return to the past is possible or even desirable, and that, on the contrary, it's those forced returns into the past or those illusory perpetuations that produce only what is false and another, more pernicious, kind of emptiness.

How should we then consider those moments of shock and even of a certain form of joy, since they're indubitable and impose themselves on us as essential, as equal to other modest or great illuminations simply given to us by life to help us confront its ever-thickening darkness? It's clear that such temples and churches will never be built again, that there's no use in doing so or in pretending to be able to do so. They were *common* houses, and such houses no longer exist; voices rose in them to form choirs that had exactly the same plenitude as the edifice in which the volume of their voices reverberated; nothing equivalent will ever again be heard. Will the choice thus be between boundless vociferation and chorales whose idealism is nauseating?

The fire without which these common houses would never have been built, the fire which wouldn't have been able to burn if there hadn't been a draught sucking it up towards the heights, that is, that very strange and fundamental need always to go, obstinately, towards what is highest, so that it warms and casts light on lives which, without it, are most often wretched or at least difficult, that fire would now not only have weakened but also be scattered, although sometimes jealously preserved in the secret depths of a heart, taking on all kinds of shapes until it becomes unrecognizable—and for me, it's something of this fire that I find, for example, in every poem worthy of the name. Does this mean that the Highest, the Very High if you will, although now scattered, lacking confidence or ferociously hidden, nonetheless remains no less active for us in this apparently damned world? Are these the final embers that the weakest wind could scatter, of a final fire after which would come only cold? Or will it flare up elsewhere, though no one knows where or how, perhaps because a pure mouth will become round above its remains and blow it awake? It's saying little to say that I know nothing. When such questions are asked, they perhaps also rise inside us like a flame. But with the wind blowing today . . . —at the very moment that I write these worlds, I recall the beginning of the last of Mahler's *Kindertotenlieder*: 'In such weather, in such a storm, I should never have let the children go outside . . . '; in today's wind, it's not only children who run the risk of dying. Be this as it may, I'll have found by looking at these very ancient enclosures of the Highest enough to arm my resistance against all forms of debasement and against the vertigo of the sinking ship.

The house has been emptied, the evening light
is gliding towards the bed of absence
where the tangle of streets comes to an end
through the grace of two children
the gleam on whose hair
is extinguished by the twilight sun.
And if their eyelids welcoming sleep
should start to close in the shadowy hour of noon
see how the children seek shelter
in a tale told of a prince
abducted by some genie and then carried off to a copper
    house
and of a princess at the window
letting her braided hair down to him
so that he can climb up to her.
The house has been emptied, but not of a murmured
    lament
rising like nostalgia, from what shore?

Badr Shakir al-Sayyab

THE THOUSAND AND ONE NIGHTS (2)

Our last evening in Beirut, on 8 November 2004, before we took the plane back to Paris, was spent at the house of Princess Fayza Salim al Kazhen: the place was beautiful, although no particularly rare objects seemed to be present, nor any pomp. The charm instead derived from the intimate warmth with which the place was impregnated and that was imparted to you as soon as you'd entered it. Intimate, especially, because most of the works of art hanging on the walls had been painted by the son of the house, a gifted artist who had died young and who, as one could sense, was still much present in the hearts and minds of the two women who now lived there alone, the mother and daughter. Indeed, this was surely the source of this particular warmth, of this beauty that I defined as intimate: familial love, whatever might have been the other kinds of love whose traces were also probably present there, yet more hidden.

There were only a few of us: besides our two hostesses, Guy Abela, whom Princess Fayza called, with bit of humour, her 'spiritual fiancé', and one of his own friends; there was Sarah the antiques dealer, who was passionate about the theatre and politics, and concerned like everyone there about the future of her country, and finally our faithful guides and supports, the K-s, and ourselves.

'Madame mère' still showed a thin and beautiful face beneath a thick chignon of black hair as well as a great mental liveliness, although she, an invalid, was unable to leave her armchair, not even for presiding over the dinner; and presiding is no exaggeration since one wouldn't have dared to refuse to taste a dish, each more savoury than the preceding one, that she offered us. Guy Abela, a man of high finance and diplomacy, the hero of a hundred journeys and poetic ecstasies, was evoking with brio such-and-such a moment of his many lives. I've met a few similar men, as different from me as one can be, who charm others with their loquaciousness, their extravagance and their youthfulness preserved through all the pitfalls of time; he's the author of those fervent *Caravans* which, according to their publisher, 'tell of mystic semen and shivering, the twists and turns of journeys, the fabulous processions, the happenstances of stopovers'—and this is no exaggeration.

What is surprising, for the rather shy and clumsy animals that we are in society, is that there was almost immediately around us, among us, thanks to that warmth that I've evoked, a natural current of gaiety, of light-hearted grace, of well-being—already experienced during the less intimate evening at the Ghassan Tueni's home—as, so I imagine, a very light dose of drugs could induce—and this analogy, after all, isn't so out-of-place in this half-dreamt Orient that we'd been nearing day after day.

But the dispenser of these wisps of smoke was, without a doubt, she who henceforth watches over the house and who tenderly takes care of her mother: Princess Fayza, gracefully floating from one guest to another; beautiful, a little pale, a sort of half-absent fairy who, however, doesn't forget she wants to be appealing, or who is appealing without even thinking about being appealing, indeed because of her remoteness and secretiveness. In her study, she shows me the beautiful books about the archaeology, the history and the art of Lebanon which she publishes and for which she conceives the page layout with obvious care and tastefulness; I spot on a bookshelf the poetry of Rilke in the Pléiade edition. It's thus true that poetry can still circulate, even in our shaken, crumbling world; poetry, and the grace that persists in some human beings, even those given a rough go by Fate, beneath their apparent privileges.

An evening of warm pleasure and cheer, from the beginning to the end, topped off when the princess' indefatigable mother smilingly allows herself to be pushed, in her armchair, to the big grand piano standing in the centre of the living room, where she plays, her memory only rarely faltering, melodies from her youth with her still-miraculously-agile fingers: the most charming, mischievous and touching gift before we had to leave.

All evening long, it was again as if I'd recovered my old, now-tattered children's book and had opened it, this time to the image of a wonderstruck Princess Badroulbadour surprised by Aladdin on her way to the bath, or of a Princess Parizade whose boldness will save her brothers from the spell that had changed them into stone statues. (I must have evoked this book four times in these relatively few pages: that is, more precisely, the illustrations, which, however, have no artistic value; the proof of the force with which they must have engraved themselves in the still-soft wax of my childhood mind.)

So the thread of a dream—for it's only a dream, but dreams belong to reality in their own ways—woven far away on the looms of India or Persia has seemingly led all the way to our more or less grey little lives, elucidating them, gilding their fabric from our childhoods; and now I've recovered its trace in my old age. The most beautiful thing is that these dreams were not always lies; that places one could visit, that human beings to whom one could speak, had maintained this radiance in them. This is what was borne out for me at the end of my life as something, once again, as *real*, despite experiences, and as dignified, as pain.

Was the slight, seemingly opiated intoxication of that evening getting me a little too carried away? Was the exaltation of the amiable Monsieur Abela's *Caravans* contaminating me? No.

I'd encountered light more often beneath the foliage of our narrow garden, on mountain paths or while walking along meadows or streams. I was sure that such light hadn't lied to me. But a more ornate, more sensual light, a light more nurtured by human sap, a more opulent and tender light, that of all the 'Orientalia' written or painted in Victor Hugo's time or afterwards (and it's not for nothing that, of the three small bound volumes of Hugo that had belonged to my grandfather, it was, at the very period of time when *The Thousand and One Nights* was enchanting me, Hugo's *Orientales* that I'd read and reread, and it was not by chance that my memory, besides the poem 'Djinns' with its virtuoso racing rhythm, had retained only the name of 'Sara the bathing woman' and its beginning: 'Sara, beautiful in her indolence, / is swaying')—that kind of light, if I could carry the memory of it as far as possible, I knew that it could also help me a little—and, after all, for that issue, no help should be neglected—to still accept the world and even, indeed, let me insist upon this point, to celebrate it all the way to the threshold of one's ever-possible, more and more probable end.

Translator's Notes

[For some of these notes, I have drawn on information given by the Gallimard-Pléiade volume of Jaccottet's works. Unless otherwise noted, all translations are mine.]

Libretto

p. 3, 'For more than twenty years'. Jaccottet is writing in 1990.

p. 5, 'Aranciate, uva, panini'. The title means 'Orangeade, eggs, bread rolls'.

p. 5, Gilbert Koull (1927–2014). This friend, with whom Jaccottet had collaborated on a puppet theatre in 1944 in Lausanne, accompanied the poet on his first trip to Italy. Koull subsequently had a career as a stage director and costume designer for the theatre.

p. 5, 'young woman artist'. Lélo Fiaux (1909–64), a well-known artist who, while living in Lausanne, had a studio at which gathered students, poets and other artists. Of her, Jaccottet has written, as quoted in the

Pléiade volume (page *xliii*): 'I met her during the war; in her own way, she set the burning rose of life against the horrors of weaponry.' Also: 'Whenever I came back from Carrouge [where Gustave Roud lived], I was somewhat of a winter traveller, aided by the silent light of the moon; whenever I left [Fiaux's] studio on the place de la Palud, I'd feel the fierce sunlight behind me. I have always kept a small reserve of those embers in my pockets.'

p. 7, 'the ambiguous Mignon'. An allusion to the poem sung by Mignon in Goethe's *Wilhelm Meister's Years of Apprenticeship*, Volume 3, Chapter 1: 'Do you know the land where the lemon trees bloom?' In French, the line is well-known as 'Connais-tu le pays où fleurissent les citronniers? or 'Connais-tu le pays des citronniers en fleurs?'. The German poet and writer (1749–1832) published this four-volume book in 1795/96.

p. 7, 'false simpletons from Sologne'. Jaccottet alludes to 'Les Niais de Sologne', the title of a movement in the 'Suite in D major' of the *Second Book of Harpsichord Pieces* by Jean-Philippe Rameau (1683–1764). A note in the Pléiade volume reports that the term 'niais', at the time, referred to a man pretending to be a simpleton out of his own interests.

p. 8, 'Count Giacinto'. The Italian composer Giacinto Scelsi (1905–88). Scelsi is apparently thinking of two passages in Goethe's *Italian Journey* (1816–17) dated 13 December and 20 December (1786), where the author, quoting Winkelmann, agrees with the latter about 'being born again' and about a 'second birth' while sojourning in Rome.

p. 8, 'the tomb of Cecilia Metella'. Located on the Via Appia to honour the daughter of the consul Quintus Caecilius Metellus Creticus and the wife of Marcus Licinius Crassus, son of Marcus Crassus, who served under Julius Caesar (100 BC–44 BC). The artist Johann Heinrich Wilhelm Tischbein placed the monument in the background of his famous painting *Goethe in the Roman Campagna* (1787).

p. 9, 'All'ombra di questa quercia'. 'In the shade of this tree, Torquato Tasso, / Near the desired Laurels and death, / Silently thought once again / Of all his misfortune.' The inscription can be found on the Convent of Sant'Onofrio, on the Janiculum Hill, where Tasso died just before being crowned poet laureate. Tasso (1544–95), born in Sorrento, is famous for his long epic poem, *Jerusalem Delivered* (1581), which depicts the battles between Christians and Muslims during the First Crusade (1096–99). Goethe published his play *Torquato Tasso* in 1790.

p. 10, 'our lyrical friend'. Lélo Fiaux.

p. 12, The artist **Giuseppe Capogrossi** (1900–72), whose style, after the Second World War, evolved towards more abstraction.

p. 15, 'this Count Hyacinth'. The composer Giacinto Scelsi's first name 'Giacinto' means 'hyacinth'.

p. 19, Gustav von Aschenbach. The main character of *Death in Venice* (1912), by Thomas Mann (1875–1955). Aschenbach is an ageing famous German writer who, while staying in Venice, falls in love with a boy, Tadzio, and eventually dies. Beginning with this translation in

1946, Jaccottet would devote much of his time to translation, through the 1990s.

p. 21n, Henri-Louis Mermod (1891–1962). A Swiss publisher who published two of Jaccottet's first books, *Requiem* (1947) and *La Promenade sous les arbres* (1957), and for whom Jaccottet also worked as a translator.

p. 22, Emanuele Luzzati (1921–2007). A stage designer and book illustrator also known for his animated cartoons. According to the obituary in the *Guardian* (6 April 2007), Luzzati 'was born in Genoa of a Jewish father. In the late 1930s when Mussolini's racial laws were being widely enforced, the family moved to Switzerland. There, at the École des Beaux Arts in Lausanne, he studied and obtained a diploma.' Luzzati returned to Italy in 1947.

p. 23, 'In this little port where the Temple of Venus has been dedicated to the Virgin'. Portovenere, which also provides the title of a poem included in Jaccottet's *L'Effraie* (The Barn-Owl, 1953).

p. 25, Henri Gaberel (1915–97). Swiss poet with whom Jaccottet travelled to Sicily over the New Year holiday in 1949–1950. Two poems in *L'Effraie*, 'Agrigente' and 'Ninfa', recall this trip.

p. 25, Houbigant is a famous French perfume. Among the clients of the firm founded by Jean-François Houbigant in 1775 were Napoleon and Queen Victoria.

p. 25, 'there's a poem by Ungaretti evoking the one in Milano'. Probably, according to the notes in the Pléiade volume, 'Dans la Galleria' (from *L'Allegria*, 1931), which is in *Vie d'un homme* (Paris: Gallimard,

1981), a translation by Jaccottet of the selected poems of Italian poet Giuseppe Ungaretti (1888–1970).

p. 28, 'Nerval's Posillipo'. An allusion to the French poet's most famous sonnet, 'El Desdichado', which begins: 'Je suis le ténébreux,—le veuf,—l'inconsolé, / Le prince d'Aquitaine à la tour abolie : / Ma seule étoile est morte, et mon luth constellé / Porte le soleil noir de la Mélancolie. // Dans la nuit du tombeau, toi qui m'as consolé, / Rends-moi le Pausilippe et la mer d'Italie . . . ' Will Stone translates: 'I am the brooding shadow— the bereaved—the unconsoled, / Aquitaine's prince of the doomed tower: / My only *star* is dead and my astral lute / Bears the *black sun* of *melancholy*. // In the sepulchral night, you who consoled me, / Give back Posillipo and the sea of Italy . . . ' (*Les Chimères*, London: Menard Press, 1999).

p. 28, The Italian artist **Andrea Mantegna** (1431–1506). Jaccottet is perhaps thinking of Mantegna's *Virgin of Victory* (*c*.1496), in which the setting is an apse formed by a pergola of leaves, flowers, fruit and birds.

p. 30, Michel and Loukie Rossier, and René and Maryse Lehmann. Friends of the Jaccottets, who took trips to Italy with them between 1974 and 1980. According to the information provided in the Pléiade volume, the 'Postcards' were originally written in a notebook that was then given to the Rossiers in appreciation for their friendship and support. Michel Rossier, an art collector, music lover and benefactor who owned a marble works in Vevey, gave financial support to numerous writers, musicians and artists. He and his wife organized trips for and with the Jaccottets (to Italy, London, Greece, and New York) up to a final one, to Italy, in June 1997. In Jaccottet's tribute to his close friend, he writes: 'Approaching the enigma of flowers is less difficult, probably, than expressing the quality of human beings, since one has scruples about touching upon it with words' (*Un humaniste dans la cite*, Vevey: Fondation pour les Arts et les Lettres, 2002).

p. 33, *The Georgics* (*c.*29 BC). A long poem about agriculture by Roman poet Virgil (70 BC–19 BC).

p. 34, The Italian artist **Antonio Allegri da Correggio** (1489–1534) was known for his sensuous, illusionist paintings. *Danaë* (*c.*1531) is housed in the Borghese Gallery in Rome and in it, Danaë lies on a bed while Eros is pulling away the sheet covering her spread thighs.

p. 35, 'as those gems did for Novalis' miners'. The German Romantic poet Novalis (1772–1801) was a mining engineer.

p. 36, The Gonzagas. Or the House of Gonzaga, a princely family who ruled in Mantua and, more generally, in Northern Italy from 1328 to 1708. In the Ducal Palace, itself a kind of 'maze' of gardens, galleries, chapels and courtyards, the 'Camera degli Sposi' or 'Bridle Chamber' was frescoed by Mantegna between 1465 and 1474. English readers will remember that the play within the play (Act 3, Scene 2) in *Hamlet* is titled *The Murder of Gonzago*, or *The Mousetrap*.

p. 37, 'like Carpaccio's monks running off from Saint Jerome's nonetheless kindly lion'. Vittore Carpaccio's painting *Saint Jerome and the Lion* (1502), kept in the Schula di San Giorgio degli Schiavoni in Venice.

Carpaccio (1465–1525 or 1526) is known for his narrative paintings and is associated with the Venetian school.

p. 37, 'The Duke Élie'. The Palazzo Contarini dal Zaffo, also known today as the Palazzo Polignac, was the abode of Winnerita Singer, the Princess of Polignac and the daughter of Isaac Merritt Singer, who founded the famous sewing machine firm. Élie was the great grandnephew of the Princess of Polignac.

p. 38, 'a cruel story of Doges'. Giuseppe Verdi's opera *Simon Boccanegra*, first performed at La Fenice in 1857.

p. 38, 'San Zaccaria'. A monastic church in Venice. The painting evoked here, according to the Pléiade volume, is probably Giovanni Bellini's *Sacred Conversation* altarpiece (1505). While the Virgin Mary, the Christ child and the four saints—Peter, Jerome, Catherine of Alexandria and Lucy—are playing no musical instrument, an angel is playing a violin or a viola at their feet.

p. 39, Simone Martini (1284–1344). The Italian artist, painted miracles such as *The Miracle of the Child falling from the Balcony* (*c.*1328), which is found in the lower section of the left panel of a triptych in the Church of St Augustine Novello in Sienna. This wood panel is, arguably, what Jaccottet is thinking of in his analogy.

p. 40, 'a tireless faux-Brendel'. A reference to the Austrian pianist Alfred Brendel (b. 1931).

p. 42, *The Baptism of Christ* (1448–50) by Piero della Francesca (*c.*1412/20–92).

p. **46**, 'building also called the Arsenal, yet banally modern and camouflaged in green and grey'. A text in *La Semaison*, dated March 1973, evokes 'the Arsenal, blind behind its grille'. The translation of this line is by Tess Lewis (*Seedtime*, London: Seagull Books, 2013, p. 234.) The Arsenal was located in Moudon, Switzerland, the poet's hometown.

p. **46**, 'Quale nell'arzanà de'Viniziani / bolle l'inverno la tenace pece / a rimpalmare i legni non sani'. *Inferno*, Canto 21, 7–9. 'As in the arsenal of the Venetians / boils in winter the tenacious pitch / to caulk the damaged boats'.

Crystal and Smoke

THE WORDS 'ANDALUSIAN', 'ANDALUSIA' . . .

p. **52**, Francisco de Goya (1746–1828). Spanish painter. Jaccottet is probably thinking of his *The Sleep of Reason Produces Monsters*, an etching from the series *Los Caprichos* (1799).

p. **53**, Ronda, Spain. Suffering from an existential crisis in December 1912, and unable to continue working on the *Duino Elegies*, the German poet Rainer Maria Rilke (1875–1926) took a trip from Paris to Spain, where he visited Toledo, Cordova and Seville. He then went to Ronda, where he stayed at the Hotel Reina Victoria and wrote 'The Spanish Trilogy' in early January 1913. Note the first lines of the first part of this poem, which, arguably, evoke the same landscape that Jaccottet sees from his hotel room: 'From this cloud—look: that so wildly covers / the star that just shone there—(and from me), / from these mountains across the way, which hold / night, nightwinds, for a while—(and from me), / from this stream on the valley's floor, which catches / the gleam of torn sky-clearings—(and from me) . . . ' (*Uncollected Poems: Rainer Maria Rilke*, Edward Snow trans., New York: Farrar, Straux and Giroux, 1996). Jaccottet is an eminent translator of Rilke's work into French and author of *Rilke par lui-même* (Paris: Éditions du Seuil, 1970).

p. 53, Federico García Lorca (1898–1936). Spanish poet and an attentive reader of Góngora. In *Lorca: An Appreciation of His Poetry* (New Haven: Yale University Press, 1952, pp. 17–18), Roy Campbell deals with the same imagery that interests Jaccottet:

> Here is a fragment of [Góngora's] *Soledad*, which almost forms a *casida* in itself for sheer figurative brilliance. All it wishes to say is that the sun was entering the sign of the Bull:
>
>> The year its flowery station reached, and now
>> Europa's robber, in a shape that lied,
>> (A crescent moon the weapons of his brow,
>> The Sun the shining bristles of his hide)
>> Refulgent pride of heaven, as he blazed,
>> On sapphire fields the gold star-clover grazed.

Again and again we come upon echoes of extreme Góngorism in Lorca—especially in such far-fetched images as when a child, seeing the full-moon reflected in the water, invites it to clash its cymbals in the comic *Ballad of Don Pedro*. But there is no image in Góngora that haunts Lorca more than that third line of the above extract:

Media luna las armas de du frente
('A crescent moon the weapons of his brow')

which is echoed at least a dozen times in different ways
in his verse. He sees even the boys who are bathing in
the evening as being charged by the waves which
reflect he crescent, as by cattle with lowered horns:

> Dense oxen of the waters charge,
> With lowered heads, the youngsters bold
> Who bathe between their crescent moons
> And undulating horns of gold.

and again in the same poem, the *Romance del
Emplazado*,

> It will be in the night, the darkness,
> By the magnetic mountain streams
> Where the oxen of the water
> Drink up the rushes in their dreams.

p. 53, Luis de Góngora y Argote (1561–1627). Spanish
poet. *Les Solitudes* (Geneva: Éditions La Dogana,
1984) and *Treize sonnets et un fragment* (Geneva: Éditions La Dogana, 1985) gather Jaccottet's selection of
Góngora's work which, at first glance, might seem
far removed from his own poetics. Jaccottet's travel
writing indeed elucidates their proximity. The image
he quotes is from Góngora's 'Second Solitude':
'And thus might we a lusty bullock find, / Young.
two-year-old—whose noble horns have now /
Hardly their crescent set upon his brow' (*The Solitudes
of Don Luis de Góngora*: *A Text with Verse Translation*
[1931], Edward Meryon Wilson trans., Cambridge:

Cambridge University Press, 2010). Note the poet José-Flore Tappy's essay 'Lire Góngora en français' in *Philippe Jaccottet* (J. P. Vidal ed., Paris: Payot, 1989, pp. 235–44).

p. 56, There are several memorable female characters in the stories (*Novelas Ejemplares*, 1613) of Miguel de Cervantes (1547–1616). Jaccottet is perhaps also thinking of the passage in *Don Quixote* (two volumes: 1605, 1615) where Don Quixote sees Lady Doña Rodríguez and at first thinks that she's a phantom, witch or sorceress. When he recognizes her, he asks: 'Tell me, Lady Doña Rodríguez (. . .) your grace has not by chance come here to practice some sort of matchmaking?' (James H. Montgomery trans., Indianapolis, IN: Hackett Classics, p. 676).

p. 57, 'the fruit that is the town emblem'. The pomegranate is the symbol of the city of Granada, where the Alhambra is found.

p. 59, Lorca's lines are from his poem 'The Ballad of the Spanish Civil Guard'.

CRYSTAL AND SMOKE

p. 61, 'The virgin, vivid, and lovely today'. The title of a well-known sonnet by Mallarmé (1842–98): 'Le vierge, le vivace et le bel aujourd'hui / Va-t-il nous déchirer avec un coup d'aile ivre / Ce lac dur oublié que hante sous le givre / Le transparent glacier des vols qui n'ont pas fui . . . ' ('Will the virgin, vivid and lovely today / Tear us with a drunken flap of its wing / This harsh forgotten lake that beneath the frost / Is haunted by the transparent glacier of flights that haven't fled . . . ').

p. 63, The military stronghold of **Mycenae** goes back to the second millennium BC whereas the Greek playwright Aeschylus lived between *c.*526 and 456 BC. His play 'The Eumenides' depicts how Orestes is pursued by the Erinyes—the 'Furies'—because of his murdering his mother, Clytemnestra. 'The Eumenides', 'The Libation Bearers' and 'Agamemnon' form the trilogy *The Oresteia.*

p. 67, A. E. is the pseudonym of George Russell (1867–1935). Jaccottet writes about the mystical ideas of this Irish poet, artist, and nationalist in *La Promenade sous les arbres* (1957).

p. 68, George Seferis (1900–71). Greek poet, noted for evoking the spirit of place.

p. 68, 'For it will be made of pure light alone'. Lines by Baudelaire from the end of his poem 'Bénédiction':

Car il ne sera fait que de pure lumière,
Puisée au foyer saint des rayons primitifs,
Et dont les yeux mortels, dans leur splendeur
    entière,
Ne sont que des miroirs obscurcis et plaintifs!

For it will be made of pure light alone,
Drawn from the holy hearth of primitive rays,
Of which mortal eyes, in all their splendor,
are but dimmed and doleful mirrors!

p. 68, Friedrich Hölderlin (1770–1843). German poet whose verse is often cited by Jaccottet. The adjective 'heilig-nüchtern' is found in his poem 'Hälfte des Lebens' ('Half of Life'): ' . . . Ihr holden Schwäne, / Und trunken von Küssen / Tunkt ihr das Haupt / Ins heilignüchterne Wasser' (' . . . Sweet swans, / Drunk with kisses, / You dip your heads / Into the holy, sober water'). The lines beginning 'O land of Homer! . . .' are found in his poem 'Die Wanderung':

> O Land des Homer !
> Am purpurnen Kirschbaum oder wenn
> Von dir gesandt im Weinberg mir
> Die jungen Pfirsiche grünen,
> Und die Schwalbe fernher kommt und vieles
>   erzählend
> An meinen Wänden ihr Haus baut, in
> Den Tagen des Mais, auch unter den Sternen
> Gedenk ich, o Ionia, dein! . . .

p. 69, Osip Mandelstam (1891–1938). Russian poet whom Jaccottet has also translated: see *Simple promesse* (Geneva: Éditions La Dogana, 1994) for Jaccottet's translations of Mandelstam's poetry, alongside other translations made by Louis Martinez and Jean-Claude Schneider. The lines quoted here are from the poem No. 116 in *Tristia* and dated November 1920.

p. 70, The reference to a 'calm fire' in Hölderlin's long-poem 'Patmos' (written in 1803, first published in 1808) is found in the third stanza: 'Und voll von Blumen der Garten, / Ein stilles Feuer'. By adding 'is ablaze', I'm following Jaccottet's vivid interpretation in French, which adds 'flamboie': 'où gorge de fleurs le jardin flamboie, un calme feu'. A longer excerpt appears at the beginning of *A Calm Fire*.

p. 70, 'Helen and the swans of the Eurotas river'. Zeus turned himself into a swan and raped Leda, who was bathing in the Eurotas river. Leda then gave birth to Helen.

p. 70, François-René de Chateaubriand (1768–1848). French writer and political figure. His *Itinéraire de Paris à Jérusalem* was published in 1811 and recounts his trip between July 1806 and June 1807. His prose epic *Les Martyrs* was published in 1809.

p. 74, 'the grain of deep and perfect faith'. Mandelstam's line, sometimes translated as 'the grain of whole and perfect faith', is the last line of the poem No. 124, dated 1921, in *Tristia*.

p. 75, Pindar (518–438), Greek poet. The story of the. sparing of his house, by Alexander, is told variously by Arrian, Plutarch, Aelian, Dio Chyrsostom, Pliny the Elder and others.

p. 76, Colonus. *Oedipus at Colonus*, by Sophocles (*c*.497–6 BC–406–5 BC) written shortly before his death. As the play opens, Oedipus appears as a blind beggar. Accompanied by his daughter, Antigone, he learns that he has arrived at Colonus. Ismene, his other daughter, arrives from Thebes.

p. 78, Hesiod (active between 750 and 650 BC) wrote his *Works and Days* around 700 BC. The lines beginning 'Poor idiots . . . ' are lines 40–1 in the poem. The lines beginning 'But when the snail . . . ' are lines 571–4.

p. 80, Hesiod's lines beginning 'May your feet not cross the beautiful waves' are lines 737–9 in *Works and Days*.

p. 86, Fourvière Hill. A prominent hill in the city of Lyon. Located just west of the old town and rising abruptly from the Saône river.

p. 87, Imru' al-Qais. Arabic poet (sixth century AD) and often considered the father of Arabic poetry. Armand Robin (1912–61) was French poet, writer and especially a famous translator who rendered works from at least twenty-two languages. Here I've translated, from the French, his 're-invention' of Imru' al-Qais's Arabic.

p. 90n, 'King of all rivers'. In Spanish: ' del Rey corona de los otros ríos: / en cuya orilla el viento hereda ahora / pequeños no vacíos / de funerales bárbaros trofeos / que el Egipto erigió a sus Ptolomeos'. The translation (of lines 953–7 of *First Solitude*) is from *Selected Poems of Luis de Góngora* (John Dent-Young trans., Chicago: University of Chicago Press, 2007). Note that Jaccottet interprets these lines somewhat differently: 'roi de tous les fleuves . . . au bord duquel le vent n'hérite plus / Que les vastes absences / de ces funèbres barbares trophées / par l'Égypte à ses princes consacrés'. In English, as adapted from Jaccottet's French: 'the king of all rivers . . . on whose banks the wind inherits nothing more / than the vast absences / of these barbaric funeral trophies / dedicated by Egypt to its princes'.

p. 92, Nicolas Poussin (1594–1665). French artist whose painting *Summer*, housed at the Louvre, is one of a series of four canvases (1660–64) devoted to the seasons.

p. 93, 'Rebecca stopping once again near a well'. See Genesis 24, Abraham was seeking a wife for his son Isaac. Abraham's servant, ordered to seek out this bride, devises a test: he stands near the well and prays to God that he will choose the one who first comes and offers water to both him and his camels. Rebecca appears and fulfils this task.

REMARKS

p. 96, 'Landscape of Laments'. In the tenth and last *Duino Elegy*, Rilke uses the noun 'Klage' (Lament) several times and in various ways. Jaccottet is thinking of a long passage where the poet evokes a 'Landschaft der Klagen' (Landscape of Laments or Lamentation) through which he's led by woman in the form of a 'youthful Lament': 'Gently she leads him across the wide Landscape of Lamentation, / shows him the columns of temples and the ruins of / castles from which, long ago, the Lords of Lament / wisely governed the land. Shows him the towering / Tear Trees and fields of flowering Melancholy / (known to the living only as tender foliage); / shows him the grazing beasts of Grief, and at times a / bird is startled and scrawls as it flies low through their upward / gaze the far-reaching scroll of its solitary cry. At / dusk she. leads him out to the graves of the elders / of the House of Lament, the Sibyls and Seers. / Night drawing near, they move more softly, and soon / it rises moon-like before them, the guardian / monument, brother to that on the Nile, / the majestic Sphinx: the face of the secret / chamber. / And they marvel at the regal head which once and for all / silently placed the face of man / on a par with the stars.' Rainer Maria Rilke, *Duino Elegies*

(Patrick Bridgwater trans., London: Menard Press, 1999, pp. 75–6).

p. 96, 'just after arriving in Paris'. Jaccottet moved to Paris towards the end of September 1946. The Pléiade volume indicates (p. *xlv*) that he corresponded at the time with his former ancient Greek professor, André Bonnard, about the meaning of poetry with respect to death.

p. 97, Gustave Roud (1897–1976). Swiss poet and shortprose writer who exerted an important influence on Jaccottet. Jaccottet's study *Gustave Roud* was published by Éditions Seghers in 1968, then expanded for a new edition by Éditions Universitaires de Fribourg in 1982. See also Philippe Jaccottet and Gustave Roud, *Correspondance 1942–1976* (José-Flore Tappy ed., Paris: Gallimard, 2002).

p. 98, The German philosopher **Martin Heidegger** (1889–1976) writes (in 1962) about Hölderlin and the island of Delos in *Aufenthalte* [*Sojourns* (New York: SUNY Press, 1989)].

p. 105, *The Desert of the Tartars*. This novel, titled *Il deserto dei Tartari* (1940) in the original Italian, was written by Dino Buzzati (1906–72). The translator Stuart Hood calls it *The Tartar Steppe* in English. See the. edition published by David R. Godine in 1995.

p. 109, Osiris. Egyptian god and mythical king of Ancient Egypt, inventor of agriculture and religion. Murdered by his brother Seth who then drowned his dismembered body in the Nile. But his sisters Isis and Nephtys used their magical power to heal and revive him. He thereafter reaches the Beyond.

Beginning with the Word 'Russia'

BEGINNING WITH THE WORD 'RUSSIA'

p. 112, Pierre and Olga Morel. Pierre Morel (b. 1944), a friend of Jaccottet's, was the French ambassador to Russia from 1992 to 1996, and invited Jaccottet for readings in St Petersburg and Moscow in May, 1996. But these three texts about Russia had already been written. Olga Bazanoff, who is also a French diplomat, is Pierre Morel's wife.

p. 113, Jules Verne (1828–1905). French novelist. The Hetzel edition of his novels remains the famous one. For *Michel Strogoff* (1876), the drawings were made by Jules Frérat and engraved by Charles Barbant. Jaccottet compares it to *The Three Musketeers* (1844) by French novelist Alexandre Dumas (1802–70).

p. 114, The German artist Max Ernst (1891–1976) used illustrations from Verne's novels for his collages in *Une semaine de bonté* (Paris: Éditions Jeanne Buchet, 1934). In English, see *Une semaine de bonté*: *A Surrealistic Novel in Collage* (New York: Dover, 1976).

p. 115, *Petrushka* (1910–11, revised 1947). Ballet by Russian composer Igor Stravinsky (1882–1971) about the loves of three puppets. The setting is the Shrovetide Fair in St Petersburg.

p. 116, James Fenimore Cooper (1789–1851). Wrote several novels about Indians, notably *Leatherstocking Tales* consisting of five books: *The Deerslayer* (1841), *The Last of the Mohicans* (1826), *The Pathfinder* (1840), *The Pioneers* (1823), and *The Prairie* (1827). *White Fang* (1906) was written mostly from the dog's viewpoint by Jack London (1876–1916).

p. 118, 'Rilke's *Book of Hours*'. *Das Stundenbuch* (1905), based in part on his two trips to Russia, with Lou-Andreas Salomé, in the summers of 1899 and 1900, and his fascination with the country.

p. 119, Anton Chekhov (1860–1904) published his story 'Easter Eve' in 1886.

p. 119, 'Mermod's Russian wife': Véra Deborah Machline.

p. 119, Charles Ferdinand Ramuz (1878–1947). The best-known Swiss novelist when Jaccottet was coming to age as a writer.

p. 120n, 'Tolstoy's *Resurrection*'. Lev Nikolayevich Tolstoy (1828–1910) published his novel *Resurrection* in 1899.

p. 122, Swiss tenor Hugues Cuénod (1902–2010). Famous for his role as the evangelist in *St Matthew Passion* (1727) by Johann Sebastian Bach (1685–1750). He recorded the *Passion* under the direction of Ernest Ansermet.

p. 122, The phrase 'Und ging heraus, und weinete bitter-lich' means, as Jaccottet translates a little farther on, 'And he went out, and wept bitterly' (Matthew 26:75). See also Luke 22:62 and Mark 14:72.

p. 124, 'the cock's crow which, in German, in Luther's German, truly creaks like an iron door'. In the original German libretto: 'Und alsbald krähete der Hahn'.

DOSTOYEVSKY: A FEW NOTES IN THE MARGINS

p. 125, 'One might think of Rembrandt'. The use of light by Rembrandt (*c*.1606/07–69) is also a preoccupation for Jaccottet in *Paysages avec figures absentes* (Paris: Gallimard, 1970).

p. 126, 'The *De Profundis*'. In Jaccottet's original French text, he cites the French translation of Blaise de Vigenère: 'De ces lieux profonds égarés, j'ai crié à toi Seigneur Dieu' and uses a different numbering system for Psalm 130, calling it Psalm 129. In the King James Version, this is Psalm 130. The Latin version begins: 'De profundis clamavi ad te, Domine'.

p. 126, Boris de Schloezer (1881–1969). A Russian settled in France in the 1920s, translator of books by Fyodor Dostoyevsky (1821–81) as well as Russian philosopher Lev Shestov (1866–1938), whose *Athènes et Jérusalem* (1937) is particularly well-known among the French writers and poets of Jaccottet's generation. In 2011, Antoine Jaccottet, the poet's son, republished Shestov's book at his press, Les Éditions Le Bruit du temps, with a postface by Yves Bonnefoy. Dostoyevsky's novel, originally published in 1864, was in fact also translated by André Markowicz, in French, as *Les Carnets du sous-sol* (Paris: Actes Sud, 1992). In 1956, it was translated as *Le Sous-Sol* by Pierre Pascal (Paris: Gallimard-Pléiade). In English, the novel has variously been called *Notes from Underground*, *Notes from the Underground*, *Letters from the Underworld*. *The Idiot* first appeared in 1868/69.

p. 127, The Italian poet and philosopher Giacomo Leopardi (1798–1837) wrote his philosophical diary, *Zibaldone*, during the years 1817 to 1832 . See also Jaccottet's *The Pilgrim's Bowl* (*Giorgio Morandi*) (John Taylor trans., London: Seagull Books, 2015), p. 13, where this same passage is quoted.

p. 129, 'Oh! the drunken gnat in the inn urinal, in love with borage, and dissolved by a ray of sunlight.' From *A Season in Hell* by Arthur Rimbaud (1854–91), the final line of the poem 'Song of the Highest Tower' in the section 'Delirium, II, Alchemy of the Word'.

p. 129, *Dead Christ* (1521–22) by Hans Holbein (1497–1543) is found in the Basel Kunstmuseum and is noted for its graphic realism.

p. 130, *The Gay Science*. Also called *The Joyful Wisdom* in English, by German philosopher Friedrich Nietzsche (1844–1900). Published in 1882. The passage quoted is Section 125.

p. 131, 'the eternal thief of energies'. Rimbaud's line comes from the last strophe, in Section 9, of 'Premières communions' (1871).

p. 131, *Crucifixion of Christ* by Matthias Grünewald (*c.*1475/80–1528) is the central panel of the Isenheim Altarpiece (1512–16).

p. 132, *Dostoïevki par lui-même*, by Dominique Arban (Paris: Éditions du Seuil, 1962). A popular French series of paperbacks in which, as the title indicates, emphasis is given to the author's own words about his writings.

p. 133, 'The Poor Knight'. A ballad by Russian poet Alexander Pushkin (1799–1837).

p. 136, Dostoyevsky's last novel, *The Brothers Karamazov*, was first published as a serial in 1879–80.

p. 136, 'like the dove of Noah's Ark'. From Genesis 8:8–12.

p. 136, In Piero della Francesca's painting *The Baptism of Christ*, the dove symbolizes the Holy Spirit.

p. 136, 'at least in Henri Mongault's translation'. Jaccottet refers to *Les Frères Karamazov*, as translated by Henri Mongault in 1923. In French: 'la fange est une furie' (see III, 11—for quotation).

p. 138, 'I'm not forgetting that Lev Shestov finds Prince Myshkin cowardly'. Shestov wrote about Dostoyevsky in *Dostoyevsky, Tolstoy, and Nietzsche* (Athens, Ohio: Ohio University Press, 1969). In French, see *La Philosophie de la Tragédie, Dostoïevski et Nietzsche* (1926; Paris: Le Bruit du Temps, 2012) and *Les Révelations de la mort, Dostoïevski et Tolstoy* (1902; Paris: Plon, 1923).

DARKNESS AND COLD, HERE IS HELL

p. 140, Camille Flammarion's *L'Astronomie populaire* (1880). A well-known book, with numerous charts and engravings, which summed up what was known of the universe at the time.

p. 141, Jean-Claude Schneider (b. 1936). French poet and translator of German and Russian poetry.

p. 141, 'I was washing myself at night in the yard'. A line by Osip Mandelstam. For the title (and first line), I've used Tess Lewis' translation from *Seedtime* (p. 268). In *Selected Poems of Osip Mandelstam* (Clarence Brown and W. S. Merwin trans., New York: New York Review Books, 1973), p. 40, this line is translated as 'I was washing outside in the darkness'. Jaccottet discovered the Russian poet in 1972 through Nadejda

Mandelstam's memoirs (*Hope against Hope*) and Mandelstam's *Voyage in Armenia* translated into French that year by the poet André du Bouchet and his son Gilles du Bouchet. Jaccottet's remark about Mandelstam's poetry striking him 'like a meteor' is found in his article 'Quelques notes à propos de Mandelstam', *La Revue de Belles-Lettres*, 1(4) (1981); republished in Jaccottet's *Une transaction secrete* (Paris: Gallimard, 1987).

p. 141, Simone Weil (1909–43). French philosopher. The words quoted here are from her *Cahiers* (Paris: Plon, 1970), p. 130.

p. 142, 'Ramuz had considered to be 'The Great Spring'. Ramuz published the essay 'Le Grand Printemps' in 1917.

p. 143, 'Yenisei river'. The largest river system flowing into the Arctic Ocean. Originating in Mongolia, the river flows northwards and drains Central Siberia.

p. 144, Ariane Efron, *Lettres d'exil 1948–1957* (Simone Luciani trans., Paris: Albin Michel, 1988). Efron (1912–75). Daughter of Serge Efron and poet Marina Tsvetaeva, she lived in France but decided to return to the Soviet Union in 1937. According to Simone Goblot, writing in *Europe* 890–1 (June–July 2003), Efron was arrested and imprisoned in 1939, forced to confess to crimes she hadn't committed and then sentenced to eight years of 're-education through work'. After eight years in a camp, she was released. She remained in semi-liberty for eighteen months but was arrested again and eventually sent to Turukhansk, not far from the Arctic Circle. She was finally released in 1955.

p. 145, Varlam Shalamov (1907–82). Russian journalist and writer who survived the Gulag and wrote *The Kolyma Tales*, a series of 147 short stories about captivity. The stories, drafted between 1954 and 1973, appeared in the Soviet Union only in 1989. In English, see *Kolyma Tales* (John Glad trans., London: Penguin, 1994).

p. 146, 'I then remembered Dante's *Inferno*'. In the French original, Jaccottet offers his own translations of *Inferno* by Dante Alighieri (1265–1321). The 'triste trou' or 'sad hole' ('tristo buco') to which Jaccottet refers is found in Canto 32, line 2. The next two tercets are from the same canto, lines 22–4 and 49–51 respectively. The 'crystal vizors' ('visiere di cristallo') comes from Canto 33, line 98. The translations of the two tercets are borrowed from Mark Musa's version (Penguin, 2003).

p. 147, 'this passage, which, at the very end of *Inferno*'. Canto 34, lines 127–34, in Mark Musa's translation.

Israel : *Blue Notebook*

p.155, Like Lev Berinsky, Jaccottet translated Rilke's. and—this is less known—Marc Chagall's poems: *Poèmes* (Geneva: Cramer, 1968).

p. 157, 'During his visit in 1806, Chateaubriand writes'. From his *Itinéraire de Paris à Jérusalem*.

p. 162, 'the story of Solomon and the Queen of Sheba'. From 1 Kings 10: 'And when the queen of Sheba heard of the fame of Solomon, concerning the name of the Lord, she came to prove him with hard questions. And she came to Jerusalem with a very great train, with camels that bare spices, and very much gold, and precious stones: and when she was come to Solomon, she communed with him of all that was in her heart . . . ' See also 2 Chronicles 9.

p. 167, 'the whip raised against the merchants of the Temple'. See Matthew 21:12 and John 2:15.

p. 168, 'Yitzhak Rabin was assassinated by a Jewish student'. Yitzhak Rabin (1922–95), the prime minister of Israel, was assassinated on 4 November 1995 by right-wing extremist Yigal Amir, who was opposed to the signing of the Oslo Accords.

p. 169, 'the market of Muristan'. A complex of streets and shops in the Christian quarter of Old Jerusalem.

p. 169, 'as though the eight-line stanzas of *Jerusalem Delivered* were being recited between two hostile and more or less degenerated liturgies.' In *Jerusalem Delivered*, Tasso depicts Clorinda as a warrior-maiden who fights on the side of the Muslims. Tancred is a Christian knight who falls in love with her. One night, she sets the Christian siege tower on fire. Tancred mistakenly kills her, but she converts to Christianity before dying.

p. 170, 'Bethseda, the pool of five porches'. From Rimbaud's *Proses évangéliques*, first published by Paterne Berrichon in *La Revue blanche* on 1 September 1897. The poem is inspired by the same passage, from the Gospel of John, which is cited just beforehand.

p. 171, 'But the observant man / saw God's face . . . ' From Friedrich Hölderlin's 'Patmos'. Jaccottet quotes from fragments of a later version of this long poem, and for my translation I have returned to the original German in Hölderlin's *Sämtliche Gedichte* (Jochen Schmidt ed., Berlin: Deutscher Klassiker Verlag, 2005), p. 359.

p. 172, 'Caspar David Friedrich's *Shipwreck*'. The German painter Caspar David Friedrich (1774–1840), whose oil painting *Die gescheiterte Hoffnung* (1823–24), literally, 'The Shattered Hope', is variously called *The Wreck of Hope* or *The Sea of Ice* in English. Jaccottet titles it *Naufrage* here, whence *Shipwreck*. The painting evokes the wreck of the *HMS Griper*, one of the two ships that took part in William Perry's 1819–20 and 1824 expeditions to the North Pole.

p. 173, 'made me think of Basilio'. Basilio is the music teacher in *The Marriage of Figaro* (1786) by Wolfgang Amadeus Mozart (1756–91).

p. 173, 'so many folk tales, especially the one about Aladdin'. 'Aladdin and his Magic Lamp' is a Middle Eastern folk tale and is included in *The Book of One Thousand and One Nights*. Not a part of the original Arabic corpus, it was added to the book in the eighteenth century by French orientalist and translator Antoine Galland (1646–1715).

p. 176, 'the prophecies of Zechariah'. In Zechariah 14:4, one reads: 'And his feet shall stand in that day upon the mount of Olives, which is before Jerusalem on the east, and the mount of Olives shall cleave in the midst thereof towards the east and towards the west, and there shall be a very great valley; and half of the mountain shall remove towards the north, and half of it towards the south.'

p. 177, 'Absalom's pillar'. See 2 Samuel 18:14.

p. 178, 'Moses saved from the river'. See Exodus 2:1–10. Poussin often painted scenes from Moses' life and especially this particular story. See, for example, *Moses Left by the River* (1624, Dresden, Gemäldegalerie Alte Meister), *The Finding of Moses* (1638, Louvre), *Moses Saved from the River* (1647, Louvre), *Moses Saved from the River* (1651, Cardiff, National Museum of Wales), and *Moses Exposed by the River* (1654, Oxford Ashmolean Museum).

p. 178, 'Moses on Mount Sinai'. See Exodus 19.

p. 178, 'Joseph deciphering dreams in Egypt'. See Genesis 37.

p. 178, 'Paul Celan mentions them in one of his last poems, because his brief stay in Israel preceded his death.' German-language poet Paul Celan (1920–70) stayed in Israel in October 1969 and committed suicide during the night of 19–20 April 1970 by jumping into the Seine from the Pont Mirabeau. In Israel, he spent time with his last lover, writer Ilana Shmueli (1924–2011). The poem evoked here is 'Die Glut' ('The Heat'): 'The Heat / counts us together / in the shriek of an ass at / Absalom's Tomb, here as well, / / Gethsemane, yonder, / circled around, whom / does it overwhelm? / / At the nearest gate nothing opens up, / / through you, Open one, I bear you to me.' Translated by John Felstiner in *The Selected Poems and Prose of Paul Celan* (New York: Norton, 2001), p. 356. The second reference here is to Celan's poem 'Der Königsweg hinter der Scheintür' ('The King's Way behind the false door'), which can be found on p. 365 of Felstiner's translation.

p. 178, 'Now Absalom in his lifetime '. See 2 Samuel 18:18.

p. 184, 'Saul's great battle against the Philistine'. See 1 Samuel 31: 1–4.

p. 184, 'Ye mountains of Gilboa'. See 2 Samuel 21.

p. 185, 'I am distressed for thee'. See 2 Samuel 6.

p. 185, 'The story of the death of Saul'. See 1 Samuel 31 and 2 Samuel 1.

p. 185, 'those epic tales'. The etymology of the French word 'épopée(s)' ('epic'), which I have translated as 'epic tale(s)', is the Greek 'epopoiía' ('tale in verse'), composed of 'epos' ('word') and 'poiein' ('to make').

p. 186, 'the Holy Spirit descending like a dove'. See John 1:32, Luke 3:22, and Matthew 3:16. Jaccottet especially recalls the passage from Matthew: 'And Jesus, when he was baptized, went up straightway out of the water: and, lo, the heavens were opened unto him, and he saw the Spirit of God descending like   a dove . . . '.

p. 186, 'the encounter at Emmaus'. See Luke 24:13–35.

p. 186, 'Lake Tiberias is dull like most lakes'. Lake Tiberias (the Sea of Galilee) is the site of the miracle of the multiplication of the loaves and fishes. See Matthew 14:13–21, Mark 6:30–44, and Luke 9:10–17, and John 6:1-15. For the story of Christ walking on the water of the lake, see Matthew 14:22–33, Mark 6:45–52, and John 6:16–24.

p. 187, 'the Monastery of Temptation'. A Greek Orthodox monastery built in the sixth century on the Mount of Temptation. Where Jesus fasted for forty days and nights and meditated while Satan was tempting him. See Matthew 4:8-10.

p. 188, 'that Moses [. . .] was buried.' See Deuteronomy 34:5–6: 'So Moses the servant of the Lord died there in the land of Moab, according to the word of the Lord. And he buried him in the valley in the land of Moab over against Beth-peor; but no man knoweth of his sepulchre unto this day.'

p. 188, 'In Qumran, while I was looking at the openings of caves'. It is said that the first of the Dead Sea Scroll discoveries occurred in 1947 when a young Bedouin shepherd, following a stray goat or sheep, threw a rock into a cave along the sea cliffs and heard a cracking sound: the rock had hit a ceramic pot containing the scrolls. The parable of the 'lost sheep' is found in Luke 15:3–6: 'And he spake this parable unto them, saying, What man of you, having an hundred sheep, if he lose one of them, doth not leave the ninety and nine in the wilderness, and go after that which is lost, until he find it? And when he hath found it, he layeth it on his shoulders, rejoicing. And when he cometh home, he calleth together his friends and neighbours, saying unto hem, Rejoice with me; for I have found my sheep which was lost.' See also Matthew 18:12.

p. 189, 'He looked towards Sodom and Gomorrah'. See Genesis 19:28, for the first quotation about Sodom and Gomorrah, and Genesis 19:24 for the rain of 'brimstone and fire'.

p. 189, 'a clear heat upon herbs'. See Isaiah 18:4.

p. 190, 'I will make mine arrows drunk with blood.' See Deuteronomy 32:42. See Judges 4: 21 for the story of General Sisera's murder; and Judges 16 for the story of Delilah and Samson, especially Judges 16:21.

p. 190, 'that story told at the end of the nineteenth chapter of Judges'. The story has a final verse, which isn't quoted by Jaccottet: 'And it was so, that all that saw it said, There was no such deed done nor seen from the day that the children of Israel came up out of the land of Egypt unto this day: consider of it, take advice, and speak your minds.'

p. 193, 'Saul, on the eve of a battle, consults a necromancer'. See 1 Samuel 28:12–14. Translations of this passage vary. I've used the King James Version, but I have employed the singular 'a god' instead of 'gods' to correct the error and mirror the French version used by Jaccottet where it's in fact stated: 'J'ai vu un Elohim qui montait de la terre.'

p. 194, 'in the Solomon's Song'. See Solomon's Song 6:10. In the French version used by Jaccottet, one finds: 'Qui est celle qui s'avance semblable à l'aube / Belle comme la lune blanche'. Other versions offer different interpretations of the original. Most importantly, the word for 'moon' [*lebanah*, alliterative with *Lebanon* and *lebonah* (frankincense)] is related to the word 'white' or 'whiteness'. I've adapted the text in the King James Version to underscore this parallel.

p. 198, 'I've recently discovered d'Aubigné'. Théodore Agrippa d'Aubigné (1552–1630), French writer and poet who also fought in several battles. His epic poem

Les Tragiques (1615) evokes the religious wars between the Catholics and the Protestants (on whose side d'Aubigné fought). 'The air is now but sunrays, so sown it is with Angels' is from *Les Tragiques* (VII, 720).

p. 202, 'Citis pond'. Freshwater pond in southern France.

A Calm Fire

p. 210, 'Marie and Gérard Khoury'. Close friends of the Jaccottets. Gérard Khoury (1938–2017) was a Franco-Lebanese writer, historian and a specialist of the Middle East.

p. 213, '*And quicker than I had thought*'. From Hölderlin's 'Patmos'. The title of Jaccottet's book is taken from the last line of this excerpt. Jaccottet is using Gustave Roud's French version (Hölderlin, *Poèmes*, Lausanne: La Bibliothèque des Arts, 2002). For my version, I'm consulting the text (and the variants) in Hölderlin's *Sämtliche Gedichte* (Berlin: Deutscher Klassiker Verlag, 2005), but also keeping in mind Roud's decisions, notably his line 'Tu t'ouvris à moi comme une fleur', the sensuality of which is resonates with Jaccottet's theme here.

p. 215, Ghassan Tueni (1926–2012). Editor-in-chief of *An Nahar*, a leading newspaper founded by his father Gebran Tueni in 1933. The poet Nadia Tueni (1935–83), his wife, won the Prix de l'Académie Française for her volume *Poèmes pour une histoire* (1972). Gebran Tueni (1957–2005), their son, was a prominent journalist and politician who was later assassinated.

p. 215, Georges Schehadé (1905–89). Lebanese Francophone poet and playwright.

p. 216, Dominique Fernandez (b. 1929). French travel writer, essayist, and translator (of Italian literature).

p. 218, *The Woman of Alger* (1834) by Eugène Delacroix (1798–1863) is housed in the Louvre. Set in a sumptuously decorated apartment with a nargileh, it depicts four women, three of whom are wearing sensually. billowing garments and gold jewellery. The fourth is a black slave who is leaving the scene.

p. 219, 'an awkward, yet sincere, *Requiem*'. Written in 1946, published in 1947 by Mermod. Republished in an expanded version in 1991 by Fata Morgana.

p. 221, '*In space full and empty like a ring*'. From Georges Schehadé, *Le Nageur d'un seul amour* (Paris: Gallimard, 1985).

p. 225, 'Columns: the 'Cantique' that Valéry devoted to them'. The long poem 'Cantique des colonnes', by Paul Valéry (1871–1945), originally published in his collection *Charmes* (1922). In his collection of critical essays, *La Chasse aux trésors* (Paris: Gallimard, 1992), French writer Henri Thomas (1912–93) discusses Mallarmé, Francis Ponge, and Valéry and evokes the 'disciple of spun glass'.

p. 227, Charles Corm (1894–1963). Lebanese writer and poet who mostly wrote in French.

p. 229, Fouad Gabriel Naffah (1925–83). Lebanese Francophone poet. The poem translated here, titled 'Prière', is from his first book, *La description de l'homme, du cadre* *et de la lyre*, self-published in Beirut in 1957 and then by Mercure de France in 1963.

p. 232, Ibn Jubayr (1145–1217). Explorer and travel writer. The quotation is from *Voyageurs arabes* (Paris: Gallimard-Pléiade, 1995).

p. 232, Ibn Battuta (1304–68 or 69). Like Ibn Jubayr, was an explorer and travel writer. The quotation is from *Voyageurs arabes* (Paris: Gallimard, 1995).

p. 235, Adonis (b. 1930). One of the most poetically and politically influential voices in Arab-language poetry. The poem quoted here dates to 1968. Jaccottet borrows Anne Wade Minkowski's translation from *Mémoire du vent* (Paris: Gallimard, 1991).

p. 237, 'Salsabil in Paradise'. Salsabil is an Islamic Arabic term referring to a spring, a river or a fountain in Paradise. See surah 23:50. There are countless translations of this surah. I've kept the English close to the French translation used by Jaccottet.

p. 238, 'On broad avenues like "Straight Street"'. An ancient Roman road that runs from east to west in the old city of Damascus. It was visited by Paul the Apostle. Note Acts 9:11: 'And the Lord said unto him [i. e. Ananias], Arise, and go into the street which is called Straight, and enquire in the house of Judas for one called Saul, of Taurus: for, behold, he prayeth.'

p. 242, 'the noble clemency of Harun al-Rashid'. Several tales in the *Thousand and One Nights* evoke and fictionalize Harun al-Rashid (763 or 766–809), the fifth Abbasid Caliph. His surname means 'The Just' or 'The Upright'. Art, science, and music flourished.

during his reign (786–809), which marked the peak of the Islamic Golden Age.

p. 243, Jaccottet borrows Darwish's poem from *La terre nous est étroite* (Paris: Gallimard, 2000), translated by Elias Sanbar. The English translation here is by Jeffrey Sacks (*Why Did You Leave the Horse Alone?*, New York: Archipelago Books, 2006, p. 84).

p. 246, Rilke's 'Tenth Duino Elegy', as translated by Patrick Bridgwater (*Duino Elegies*, London: Menard Press, 1999), includes these lines: 'Gently she [a Lament] leads him across the wide Landscape of Lamentation, / shows him the columns of temples and the ruins of / castles from which, long ago, the Lords of Lament / wisely governed the land . . . '.

p. 247, 'Ulysses, facing Nausicaa [. . .] the trunk of a young palm tree'. See *Odyssey*, VI, 162–3: 'Of a truth in Delos once I saw such a thing, a young shoot of a palm springing up beside the altar of Apollo . . . ' (*Vol. 1*, A. T. Murray trans., Cambridge, MA: Harvard University Press, 1919).

p. 248, 'Hölderlin's famous "Song of Fate".' 'Hyperions Schicksalslied', from the second volume of his epistolary novel *Hyperion oder Der Eremit in Griechenland* (Hyperion or the Hermit in Greece, 1799).

p. 250, 'Ages of Life'. Hölderlin's 'Lebensalter', written in 1803–04. The phrase 'Wohleingerichteten Eichen', which Jaccottet translates as 'les chênes en belle ordonnance', is cited elsewhere in his writings. Here, it is rendered in Nick Hoff's translation (*Odes and Elegies*, Middletown, CT: Wesleyan University Press, 2008,

p. 180) as 'a pleasant stand of oak'. It can be thought of as a 'well-ordered array of oaks'.

pp. 252–3, 'Guarded by silence and courtesy'. From *Amers* (1957) by French poet Saint-John Perse (1887–1975).

p. 255, Salah Stétié (b. 1929). French poet originally from Lebanon. Jaccottet takes this poem from *L'autre côté brûlé du très pur* (Paris: Gallimard, 1992).

p. 259, The Mandelstam quotations are from his *Selected Essays* (Sidney Monas trans., Austin: University of Texas Press, 1977), p. 202.

p. 268, 'the rest of us, Eliot's "hollow men".' 'The Hollow Men' (1925) by T. S. Eliot (1888–1965), begins: 'We are the hollow men / We are the stuffed men / Leaning together / Headpiece filled with straw. Alas! / Our dried voices, when / We whisper together / Are quiet and meaningless / As wind in dry grass / Or rats' feet over broken glass / In our dry cellar . . . ' It ends: '*This is the way the world ends / Not with a bang but a whimper.*'

p. 270, 'Mahler's *Kindertotenlieder*'. A song cycle by Gustav Mahler (1860–1911), composed in 1904 and using poems by Friedrich Rückert.

p. 271, Badr Shakir al-Sayyab (1926–64). Iraqi poet. Jaccottet takes this poem from *Les poèmes de Djaykoûr* (Salah Stétié and Kadhim Jihad trans, Montpellier: Fata Morgana, 2000). This is actually the last stanza, beginning on line 23, of the poem 'Khala al-bayt' (The House is Deserted).

p. 273, Guy Abela (1929–2015). Lebanese francophone poet. His book *Caravans* was published in 1983.

p. 274, 'the K-s'. The Jaccottets' close friends, the Khourys, to whom *A Calm Fire* is dedicated.

p. 277, *Les Orientales* (1829) by Victor Hugo is a volume of poems well known for their evocations of the Mediterranean Middle East and, specifically, for the poem 'Djinns', which has fifteen stanzas organized syllabically in a virtuoso manner.